U0877275

新曲綫 New Curves | 用心雕刻每一本......

http://site.douban.com/110283/
http://weibo.com/nccpub

用心字里行间　雕刻名著经典

Human Resource Management

Tenth Edition

O.C. Ferrell
University of New Mexico

Geoffrey A. Hirt
DePaul University

Linda Ferrell
University of New Mexico

人力资源管理

第10版

双语教学版

O.C. 费雷尔
［美］杰弗里·赫特　著
琳达·费雷尔

人民邮电出版社
北　京

图书在版编目（CIP）数据

人力资源管理：第 10 版：双语教学版：汉、英 /（美）O.C. 费雷尔等著 .
-- 北京：人民邮电出版社，2018.3（2023.7 重印）
商务英语 / 工商管理双语教学教材系列
ISBN 978-7-115-47599-2

Ⅰ . ①人…　Ⅱ . ① O…　Ⅲ . ①人力资源管理 – 双语教学 – 教材 – 汉、英　Ⅳ . ① F243

中国版本图书馆 CIP 数据核字（2018）第 004635

O.C. Ferrell, Geoffrey A. Hirt, Linda Ferrell
Human Resource Management, 10th Edition
ISBN 978-1-259-17939-6

人力资源管理（第 10 版，双语教学版）

◆ 著　　[美] O.C. 费雷尔　杰弗里 · 赫特　琳达 · 费雷尔
策　划　刘　力　陆　瑜
责任编辑　王润秋
装帧设计　陶建胜

◆ 人民邮电出版社出版发行　北京市丰台区成寿寺路 11 号
邮编　100164　电子邮件　315@ptpress.com.cn
网址　http://www.ptpress.com.cn
电话（编辑部）010-84931398　（市场部）010-84937152
三河市少明印务有限公司印刷
新华书店经销

◆ 开本：850 × 1092　1/16
印张：7.25
字数：174 千字　　2018 年 3 月第 1 版　　2023 年 7 月第 2 次印刷
著作权合同登记号　图字：01-2017-8599

定价：38.00 元

本书如有印装质量问题，请与本社联系　电话：(010) 84937152

内容提要

《人力资源管理》（第 10 版，双语教学版）摘编自 *Business: A Changing World*（10e）一书，该书是美国同类书市场领导品牌。第一作者 O.C. 费雷尔教授，曾担任美国营销协会学术委员会主席，其研究领域包括全球商业、市场营销和商业伦理。本书主要讲述在当今商业世界的快速变化中如何打造人力资源优势，具体内容包括组织、团队和沟通，员工激励，人力资源管理和个人职业生涯规划。本书保留了原版书中全部的英文及其教材要素，编者对目录以及部分专业词汇进行了翻译。书中还引用了一些新鲜有趣的商业案例、习题，语言简练，通俗易懂。

本书可作为高等院校财经类及商务英语专业的双语课适用教材，也适用于 MBA 学员、企业管理者以及对该领域感兴趣的普通读者。

Authors 作者简介

O.C. FERRELL

O.C. Ferrell is University Distinguished Professor of Marketing and Bill Daniels Professor of Business Ethics in the Anderson School of Management at the University of New Mexico. He served as the Bill Daniels Distinguished Professor of Business Ethics at the University of Wyoming and the Chair of the Department of Marketing at Colorado State University. He also has held faculty positions at the University of Memphis, University of Tampa, Texas A&M University, Illinois State University, and Southern Illinois University, as well as visiting positions at Queen's University (Ontario, Canada), University of Michigan (Ann Arbor), University of Wisconsin (Madison), and University of Hannover (Germany). He has served as a faculty member for the Master's Degree Program in Marketing at Thammasat University (Bangkok, Thailand). Dr. Ferrell received his B.A. and M.B.A. from Florida State University and his Ph.D. from Louisiana State University. His teaching and research interests include business ethics, global business, and marketing.

Dr. Ferrell is widely recognized as a leading teacher and scholar in business. He has published more than 100 articles in leading journals. He has co-authored more than 20 books. In addition to *Business: A Changing World,* he has two other textbooks, *Marketing* and *Business Ethics: Ethical Decision Making and Cases,* that are market leaders in their respective areas. He also has co-authored other textbooks for marketing, management, business and society, and other business courses, as well as a trade book on business ethics. He chaired the American Marketing Association (AMA) ethics committee that developed its current code of ethics. He is past president of the Academic Council for the AMA. Currently he is Vice President of Publications for the Academy of Marketing Science and is a Distinguished Fellow with AMS and is the AMS, Cutco-Vector Distinguished Marketing Educator.

Dr. Ferrell's major focus is teaching and developing teaching resources for students and faculty to better understand the increasing complex global business environment. He has taught the introduction to business course using this textbook. This gives him the opportunity to develop, improve, and test the book and ancillary materials on a firsthand basis. He has traveled extensively to work with students and understands the needs of instructors of introductory business courses. He lives in Albuquerque, New Mexico, and enjoys skiing, golf, and international travel.

GEOFFREY A. HIRT

Geoffrey A. Hirt of DePaul University previously taught at Texas Christian University and Illinois State University where he was Chairman of the Department of Finance and Law. At DePaul, he was Chairman of the Finance Department from 1987 to 1997 and held the title of Mesirow Financial Fellow. He developed the MBA program in Hong Kong and served as Director of International Initiatives for the College of Business, supervising overseas programs in Hong Kong, Prague, and Manama and was awarded the Spirit of St. Vincent DePaul award for his contributions to the university. Dr. Hirt directed the Chartered Financial Analysts (CFA) study program for the Investment Analysts Society of Chicago from 1987 to 2003. He has been a visiting professor at the University of Urbino in Italy, where he still maintains a relationship with the economics department. He received his Ph.D. in Finance from the University of Illinois at Champaign–Urbana, his M.B.A. at Miami University of Ohio, and his B.A. from Ohio Wesleyan University.

Dr. Hirt is currently on the Dean's Advisory Board and Executive Committee of DePaul's School of Music and is on the Board of the James Tyree Foundation. The Tyree Foundation funds innovative education programs in Chicago, and Dr. Hirt also serves on the Grant Committee. Dr. Hirt is past president and a current member of the Midwest Finance Association, a former editor of the *Journal of Financial Education,* and also a member of the Financial Management Association. He belongs to the Pacific Pension Institute, an organization of public pension funds, private equity firms, and international organizations such as the Asian Development Bank, the IMF, and the European Bank for Reconstruction and Development.

Dr. Hirt is widely known for his textbook *Foundations of Financial Management* published by McGraw-Hill/Irwin. This book in its fifteenth edition has been used in more than 31 countries and translated into more than 14 different languages. Additionally, Dr. Hirt is well known for his textbook, *Fundamentals of Investment Management,* also published by McGraw-Hill/Irwin and now in its tenth edition. Dr. Hirt enjoys golf, swimming, music, and traveling with his wife, who is a pianist and opera coach.

LINDA FERRELL

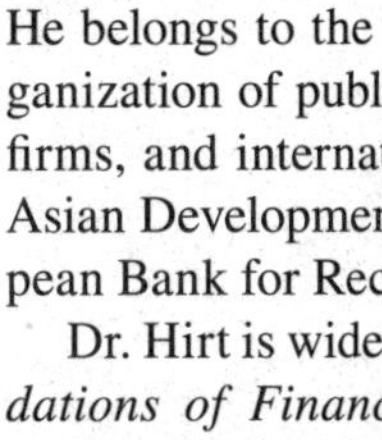

Dr. Linda Ferrell is Professor of Marketing and Bill Daniels Professor of Business Ethics in the Anderson School of Management at the University of New Mexico. She completed her Ph.D. in Business Administration, with a concentration in management, at the University of Memphis. She has taught at the University of Tampa, Colorado State University, University of Northern Colorado, University of Memphis, and the University of Wyoming. She also team teaches a class at Thammasat University in Bangkok, Thailand, as well as an online Business Ethics Certificate course through the University of New Mexico.

Her work experience as an account executive for McDonald's and Pizza Hut's advertising agencies supports her teaching of advertising, marketing management, marketing ethics, and marketing principles. She has published in the *Journal of Public Policy & Marketing, Journal of Business Research, Journal of the Academy of Marketing Science, Journal of Business Ethics, AMS Review, Journal of Academic Ethics, Journal of Marketing Education, Marketing Education Review, Journal of Teaching Business Ethics,* and *Case Research Journal,* and is co-author of *Business Ethics: Ethical Decision Making and Cases* (10th edition) and *Business and Society* (5th edition). She co-leads the Daniels Fund business ethics initiative at the University of New Mexico.

Dr. Ferrell is the President of the Academy of Marketing Science and a past president for the Marketing Management Association. She is a member of the college advisory board for Cutco Vector. She is on the NASBA Center for the Public Trust Board of Directors, University of Central Florida-Nicholson School of Communication Board of Visitors, University of Tampa-Sykes College of Business, Board of Fellows, and the Direct Selling Education Foundation Board and Executive Committee. She frequently speaks to organizations on "Teaching Business Ethics," including the Direct Selling Education Foundation's training programs, Ethics & Compliance Officer Association, NASBA Center for the Public Trust Ethical Leadership Conference, as well as others. She has served as an expert witness in cases related to advertising, business ethics, and consumer protection.

Contents 目录

Human Resource Management

1 Motivating the Workforce

员工激励

Learning Objectives

After reading this chapter, you will be able to:

- **LO 1-1** Define human relations, and determine why its study is important.
- **LO 1-2** Summarize early studies that laid the groundwork for understanding employee motivation.
- **LO 1-3** Compare and contrast the human-relations theories of Abraham Maslow and Frederick Herzberg.
- **LO 1-4** Investigate various theories of motivation, including theories X, Y, and Z; equity theory; and expectancy theory.
- **LO 1-5** Describe some of the strategies that managers use to motivate employees.
- **LO 1-6** Critique a business's program for motivating its sales force.

Chapter Outline

进入商业世界

Enter the World of Business

美国玛氏公司：一个员工热爱工作的地方

Mars, Incorporated: Where Employees Love to Work

The 70,000 employees working at Mars Inc. look forward to going to work in the morning. Mars is the third largest private company in the United States that is 100 percent family owned. The company specializes in six brand areas: chocolate, pet care, Wrigley, food, drinks, and symbioscience. While the company is known for products such as Pedigree pet care, M&Ms, and Wrigley gum, it has also become known for its motivational corporate culture. Mars has consistently made the list of *Fortune*'s "Best Companies to Work for."

Mars aims to provide a positive work environment that motivates employees to strive for excellence and provide exceptional products for consumers everywhere. To do this, Mars has stayed a private company and has no plans to go public. This keeps the company from having to answer to stockholders regarding every decision and motivates employees to develop and test new ideas. Employees fondly dub themselves "Martians" and abide by the company's Five Principles of Mars embedded on the walls of the company's offices. These principles are quality, responsibility, mutuality, efficiency, and freedom.

Employee perks at Mars are various. Employees have access to vending machines that dispense free candy, the ability to grow within the company, and the opportunity to receive bonuses from 10 to 100 percent of their salaries. Employees of the company's pet care division are encouraged to bring their dogs to work. Monitors display sales and financial updates of the company, which motivate employees to strive for success. The company has been known to employ generations of families within the firm. As a result of its motivational environment, the company boosts a low 5 percent turnover rate.[1]

引言
Introduction

Because employees do the actual work of the business and influence whether the firm achieves its objectives, most top managers agree that employees are an organization's most valuable resource. To achieve organizational objectives, employees must have the motivation, ability (appropriate knowledge and skills), and tools (proper training and equipment) to perform their jobs. Chapter 3 covers topics related to managing human resources, such as those listed earlier. This chapter focuses on how to motivate employees.

We examine employees' needs and motivation, managers' views of workers, and several strategies for motivating employees. Managers who understand the needs of their employees can help them reach higher levels of productivity and thus contribute to the achievement of organizational goals.

人际关系的本质
Nature of Human Relations

LO 1-1

人际关系
human relations
the study of the behavior of individuals and groups in organizational settings

激励
motivation
an inner drive that directs a person's behavior toward goals

What motivates employees to perform on the job is the focus of **human relations,** the study of the behavior of individuals and groups in organizational settings. In business, human relations involves motivating employees to achieve organizational objectives efficiently and effectively. The field of human relations has become increasingly important over the years as businesses strive to understand how to boost workplace morale, maximize employees' productivity and creativity, and motivate their ever more diverse employees to be more effective.

Motivation is an inner drive that directs a person's behavior toward goals. A goal is the satisfaction of some need, and a need is the difference between a desired state and an actual state. Both needs and goals can be motivating. Motivation explains why people behave as they do; similarly, a lack of motivation explains, at times, why people avoid doing what they should do. Motivating employees to do the wrong things or for the wrong reasons can be problematic, however. Encouraging employees to take excessive risks through high compensation, for example, led to the downfall of AIG and most major U.S. banks. Also, encouraging employees to lie to customers or to create false documentation is unethical and could even have legal ramifications. A person who recognizes or feels a need is motivated to take action to satisfy the need and achieve a goal (Figure 1.1). Consider a person who takes a job as a salesperson. If his or her performance is far below other salespeople's, he or she will likely recognize a need to increase sales. To satisfy that need and achieve success, the person may try to acquire new insights from successful salespeople or obtain additional training to improve sales skills. In addition, a sales manager might try different means to motivate the salesperson to work harder and to improve his or her skills. Human relations is concerned with the needs of employees, their goals and how they try to achieve them, and the impact of those needs and goals on job performance.

Many companies offer onsite day care as a benefit for employees who have children. Company benefits such as these tend to increase employee satisfaction and motivation.

Effectively motivating employees helps keep them engaged in their work. Engagement involves emotional involvement and commitment. Being engaged

FIGURE 1.1
The Motivation Process

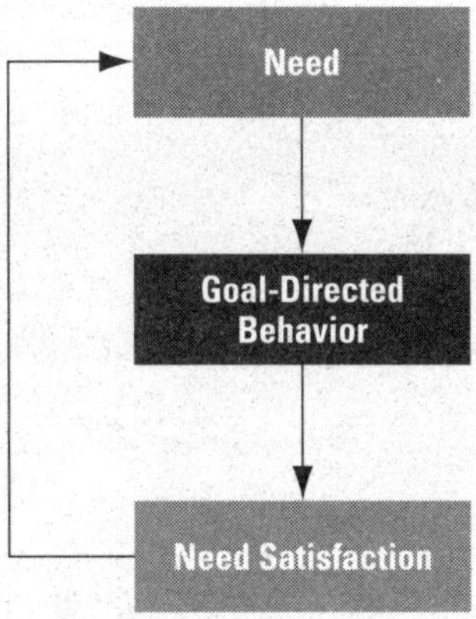

results in carrying out the expectations and obligations of employment. Many employees are actively engaged in their jobs, while others are not. Some employees do the minimum amount of work required to get by, and some employees are completely disengaged. Motivating employees to stay engaged is a key responsibility of management. For example, to test if his onsite production managers were fully engaged in their jobs, former Van Halen frontman David Lee Roth placed a line in the band's rider asking for a bowl of M&Ms with the brown ones removed. It was a means for the band to test local stage production crews' attention to detail. Because their shows were highly technical, David Lee Roth would demand a complete recheck of everything if he found brown M&Ms in the bowl.[2]

Even small symbols of recognition, such as an "Employee of the Month" parking space, can serve as strong motivators for employees.

One prominent aspect of human relations is **morale**—an employee's attitude toward his or her job, employer, and colleagues. High morale contributes to high levels of productivity, high returns to stakeholders, and employee loyalty. Conversely, low morale may cause high rates of absenteeism and turnover (when employees quit or are fired and must be replaced by new employees). Google recognizes the value of happy, committed employees and strives to engage in practices that will minimize turnover. Employees have access to onsite medical care, travel and emergency insurance, educational reimbursements, and many more incentives that keep employees' morale in good condition.[3]

Employees are motivated by their perceptions of extrinsic and intrinsic rewards. An **intrinsic reward** is the personal satisfaction and enjoyment that you feel from attaining a goal. For example, in this class you may feel personal enjoyment in learning how business works and aspire to have a career in business or to operate your own business one day. **Extrinsic rewards** are benefits and/or recognition that you receive from someone else. In this class, your grade is extrinsic recognition of your efforts and success in the class. In business, praise and recognition, pay increases, and bonuses are extrinsic rewards. If you believe that your job provides an opportunity to contribute to society or the environment, then that aspect would represent an intrinsic reward. Both intrinsic and extrinsic rewards contribute to motivation that stimulates employees to do their best in contributing to business goals.

士气
morale
an employee's attitude toward his or her job, employer, and colleagues

内在奖励
intrinsic rewards
the personal satisfaction and enjoyment felt after attaining a goal

外在奖励
extrinsic rewards
benefits and/or recognition received from someone else

TABLE 1.1
How to Retain Good Employees

1. Challenge your employees.
2. Provide adequate incentives.
3. Don't micromanage.
4. Create a work-friendly environment.
5. Provide opportunities for employee growth.

Source: Adapted from Geoff Williams, "Retaining Employees: 5 Things You Need to Know," The Huffington Post, *February 2, 2012.*

Respect, involvement, appreciation, adequate compensation, promotions, a pleasant work environment, and a positive organizational culture are all morale boosters. Table 1.1 lists some ways to retain good employees. Costco Wholesale, the second largest retailer in America, knows how to retain happy employees. The company pays an average annual rate of $20.89 per hour plus overtime, gives five weeks of vacation per year, and matches 401(k) contributions; in addition, almost 90 percent of employees are covered by company-sponsored health insurance. The retail industry is peppered with unhappy employees and dwindling profits, but Costco's efforts result in happy workers. The company was even able to give raises when the economic recession hit. In addition, the company has not experienced any major labor disputes in its more than 30 years of existence.[5] Many companies offer a diverse array of benefits designed to improve the quality of employees' lives and increase their morale and satisfaction. Some of the "best companies to work for" offer onsite day care, concierge services (e.g., dry cleaning, shoe repair, prescription renewal), domestic partner benefits to same-sex couples, and fully paid sabbaticals. Table 1.2 offers suggestions as to how leaders can motivate employees on a daily basis.

DID YOU KNOW? **Absenteeism can cost a company as much as 36 percent of payroll.[4]**

TABLE 1.2
How to Motivate Employees

1. Interact with employees in a friendly and open manner.
2. Equitably dispense rewards and other incentives.
3. Create a culture of collaboration.
4. Provide both positive and negative feedback and constructive criticism.
5. Make employees feel as if they are partners rather than workers.
6. Handle conflicts in an open and professional manner.
7. Provide continuous opportunities for improvement and employee growth.
8. Encourage creativity in problem solving.
9. Recognize employees for jobs well done.
10. Allow employees to make mistakes, as these become learning opportunities.

关于员工激励的历史观点
Historical Perspectives on Employee Motivation

LO 1-2

Throughout the 20th century, researchers have conducted numerous studies to try to identify ways to motivate workers and increase productivity. From these studies have come theories that have been applied to workers with varying degrees of success. A brief discussion of two of these theories—the classical theory of motivation and the Hawthorne studies—provides a background for understanding the present state of human relations.

古典激励理论
Classical Theory of Motivation

The birth of the study of human relations can be traced to time and motion studies conducted at the turn of the century by Frederick W. Taylor and Frank and Lillian Gilbreth. Their studies analyzed how workers perform specific work tasks in an effort to improve the employees' productivity. These efforts led to the application of scientific principles to management.

古典激励理论
classical theory of motivation
theory suggesting that money is the sole motivator for workers

According to the **classical theory of motivation,** money is the sole motivator for workers. Taylor suggested that workers who were paid more would produce more, an idea that would benefit both companies and workers. To improve productivity, Taylor thought that managers should break down each job into its component tasks (specialization), determine the best way to perform each task, and specify the output to be achieved by a worker performing the task. Taylor also believed that incentives would motivate employees to be more productive. Thus, he suggested that managers link workers' pay directly to their output. He developed the piece-rate system, under which employees were paid a certain amount for each unit they produced; those who exceeded their quota were paid a higher rate per unit for all the units they produced.

We can still see Taylor's ideas in practice today in the use of financial incentives for productivity. Moreover, companies are increasingly striving to relate pay to performance at both the hourly and managerial level. Incentive planners choose an individual incentive to motivate and reward their employees. In contrast, team incentives are used to generate partnership and collaboration to accomplish organizational goals. Boeing develops sales teams for most of its products, including commercial airplanes. The team dedicated to each product shares in the sales incentive program.

More and more corporations are tying pay to performance in order to motivate—even up to the CEO level. The topic of executive pay has become controversial in recent years, and many corporate boards of directors have taken steps to link executive compensation more closely to corporate performance. Despite these changes, many top executives still receive large compensation packages. Larry Ellison, CEO of Oracle, earns $96.2 million in annual compensation.[6]

Like most managers of the early 20th century, Taylor believed that satisfactory pay and job security would motivate employees to work hard. However, later studies showed that other factors are also important in motivating workers.

霍桑实验
The Hawthorne Studies

Elton Mayo and a team of researchers from Harvard University wanted to determine what physical conditions in the workplace—such as light and noise levels—would stimulate employees to be most productive. From 1924 to 1932, they studied a group of workers at the Hawthorne Works Plant of the Western Electric Company and measured their productivity under various physical conditions.

Going Green

Wegmans Motivates Employees and Excels in Sustainability

Wegmans, a small grocery chain along the Atlantic region, is keen on motivating its more than 42,000 employees. The 96-year-old grocer offers benefits such as flexible scheduling, employee scholarship programs, and a 66 percent rate of internal promotions to empower and motivate its workforce to optimal levels. The company generated $6.7 billion in revenue in 2013 and has been consistently ranked as one of *Fortune*'s top five best companies to work for since the list began in 1998.

Wellness programs for employees, which include free monthly health screenings, blood pressure and nutrition coaching, and onsite yoga and Zumba classes, are a priority for the chain. It will also subsidize other health programs that employees find more effective. The result is highly energized, healthy, and happy employees who feel invested in the company. Employees undergo 40 hours of training before interacting with customers and are given the opportunity to travel in order to become experts in the store's products.

Sustainability is another investment Wegmans values, and it encourages employees to feel the same. The company uses paper boats for sampling rather than plastic cups and grocery bags made from 40 percent recycled material. Wegmans retreaded the tires on its trucks rather than purchase new tires, saving more than 30,000 gallons of oil. Additionally, Greenpeace recently ranked the company number one in seafood sustainability.[7]

Discussion Questions

1. How does Wegmans empower employees?
2. Describe the employee benefits Wegmans offers and how this motivates them to offer better customer service.
3. How might Wegmans' sustainability endeavors influence employees to be more sustainable in their own lives?

Some companies let people bring their pets to work as an added incentive to make the workplace seem more friendly.

What the researchers discovered was quite unexpected and very puzzling: Productivity increased regardless of the physical conditions. This phenomenon has been labeled the Hawthorne effect. When questioned about their behavior, the employees expressed satisfaction because their co-workers in the experiments were friendly and, more importantly, because their supervisors had asked for their help and cooperation in the study. In other words, they were responding to the attention they received, not the changing physical work conditions. The researchers concluded that social and psychological factors could significantly affect productivity and morale. The United Services Automobile Association (USAA) has a built-in psychological factor that influences employee morale. The work of the financial services company serves military and veteran families, which enlivens employees. Genentech, a biotechnology company, also knows how to inspire employees through the development of medications that better the lives of patients. Patients have been known to share their stories with employees, and in one instance, employees put in extra hours to ship breast cancer medication to a hospital when they discovered three patients were awaiting treatment. This shows how important it is for employees to feel like their work matters.[8] Figure 1.2 indicates aspects of the job that appear to be most important for job satisfaction.

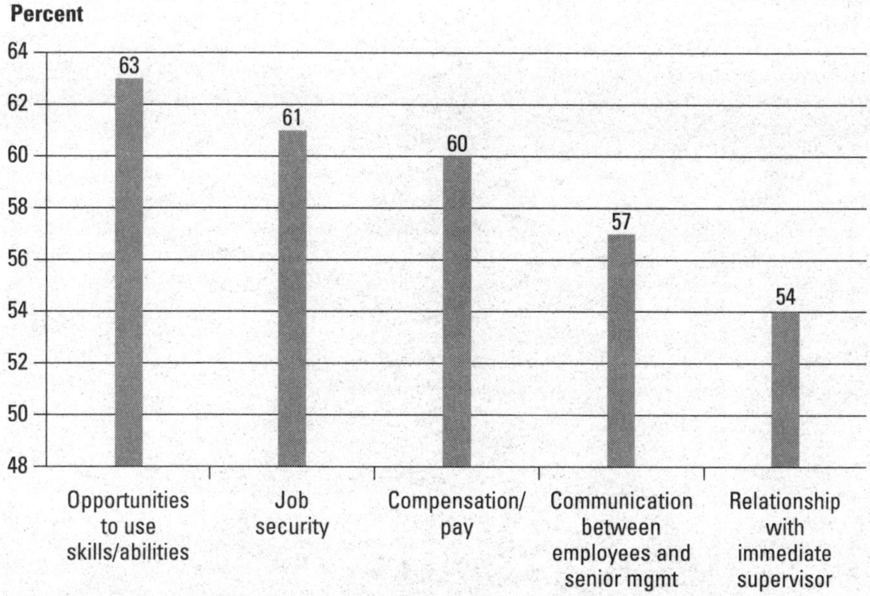

FIGURE 1.2
Job Aspects Important to Employee Satisfaction

Source: Society for Human Resource Management, 2012 *Employee Job Satisfaction and Engagement: A Research Report by SHRM.*

The Hawthorne experiments marked the beginning of a concern for human relations in the workplace. They revealed that human factors do influence workers' behavior and that managers who understand the needs, beliefs, and expectations of people have the greatest success in motivating their workers.

员工激励理论
Theories of Employee Motivation

The research of Taylor, Mayo, and many others has led to the development of a number of theories that attempt to describe what motivates employees to perform. In this section, we will discuss some of the most important of these theories. The successful implementation of ideas based on these theories will vary, of course, depending on the company, its management, and its employees. It should be noted, too, that what worked in the past may no longer work today. Good managers must have the ability to adapt their ideas to an ever-changing, diverse group of employees.

马斯洛需要层级理论
Maslow's hierarchy
a theory that arranges the five basic needs of people—physiological, security, social, esteem, and self-actualization—into the order in which people strive to satisfy them

马斯洛需要层级理论
Maslow's Hierarchy of Needs

LO 1-3

Psychologist Abraham Maslow theorized that people have five basic needs: physiological, security, social, esteem, and self-actualization. **Maslow's hierarchy** arranges these needs into the order in which people strive to satisfy them (Figure 1.3).

Physiological needs, the most basic and first needs to be satisfied, are the essentials for living—water, food, shelter, and clothing. According to Maslow, humans devote all their efforts to satisfying physiological needs until they are met. Only when these needs are met can people focus their attention on satisfying the next level of needs—security.

生理需要
physiological needs
the most basic human needs to be satisfied—water, food, shelter, and clothing

安全需要
security needs
the need to protect oneself from physical and economic harm

Security needs relate to protecting yourself from physical and economic harm. Actions that may be taken to achieve security include reporting a dangerous workplace

FIGURE 1.3
Maslow's Hierarchy of Needs

Source: Adapted from Abraham H. Maslow, "A Theory of Human Motivation," *Psychology Review* 50 (1943), pp. 370–396. American Psychology Association.

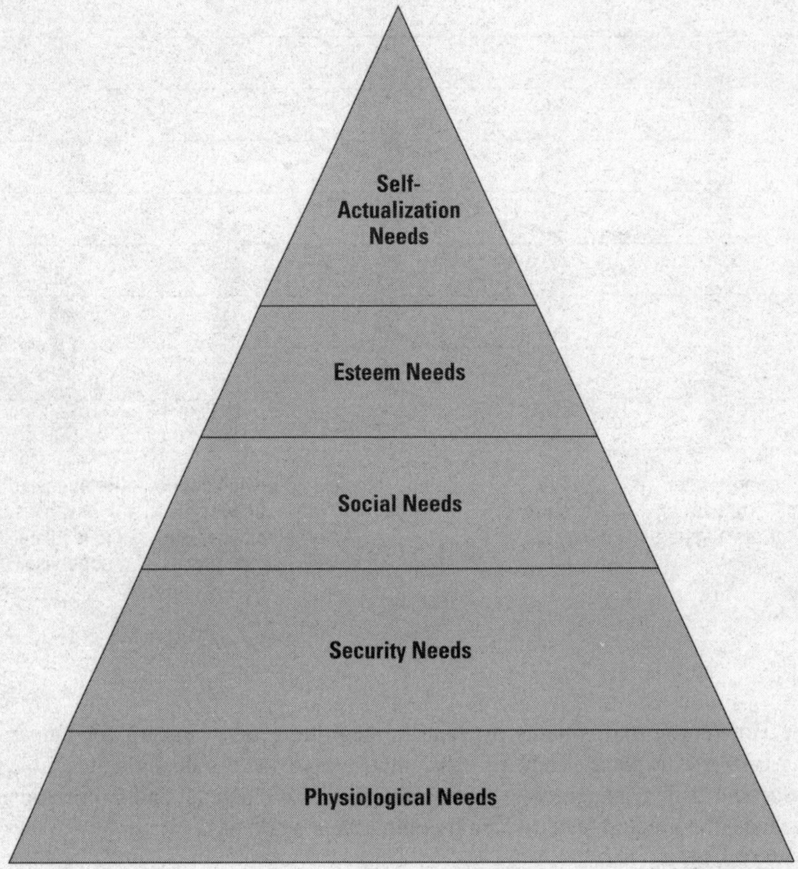

condition to management, maintaining safety equipment, and purchasing insurance with income protection in the event you become unable to work. Once security needs have been satisfied, people may strive for social goals.

社交需要
social needs
the need for love, companionship, and friendship—the desire for acceptance by others

尊重需要
esteem needs
the need for respect—both self-respect and respect from others

Social needs are the need for love, companionship, and friendship—the desire for acceptance by others. To fulfill social needs, a person may try many things: making friends with a co-worker, joining a group, volunteering at a hospital, throwing a party, and so on. Once their social needs have been satisfied, people attempt to satisfy their need for esteem.

Esteem needs relate to respect—both self-respect and respect from others. One aspect of esteem needs is competition—the need to feel that you can do something better than anyone else. Competition often motivates people to increase their productivity. Esteem needs are not as easily satisfied as the needs at lower levels in Maslow's hierarchy because they do not always provide tangible evidence of success. However, these needs can be realized through rewards and increased involvement in organizational activities. Until esteem needs are met, people focus their attention on achieving respect. When they feel they have achieved some measure of respect, self-actualization becomes the major goal of life.

Self-actualization needs, at the top of Maslow's hierarchy, mean being the best you can be. Self-actualization involves maximizing your potential. A self-actualized person feels that she or he is living life to its fullest in every way. For Stephen King, self-actualization might mean being praised as the best fiction writer in the world; for actress Halle Berry, it might mean winning an Oscar.

自我实现需要
self-actualization needs
the need to be the best one can be; at the top of Maslow's hierarchy

Maslow's theory maintains that the more basic needs at the bottom of the hierarchy must be satisfied before higher-level goals can be pursued. Thus, people who are hungry and homeless are not concerned with obtaining respect from their colleagues. Only when physiological, security, and social needs have been more or less satisfied do people seek esteem. Maslow's theory also suggests that if a low-level need is suddenly reactivated, the individual will try to satisfy that need rather than higher-level needs. Many laid off workers probably shift their focus from high-level esteem needs to the need for security. Managers should learn from Maslow's hierarchy that employees will be motivated to contribute to organizational goals only if they are able to first satisfy their physiological, security, and social needs through their work.

connect*

Need help understanding Maslow's Hierarchy? Visit your Connect ebook video tab for a brief animated explanation.

赫兹伯格的双因素激励理论
Herzberg's Two-Factor Theory

In the 1950s, psychologist Frederick Herzberg proposed a theory of motivation that focuses on the job and on the environment where work is done. Herzberg studied various factors relating to the job and their relation to employee motivation and concluded that they can be divided into hygiene factors and motivational factors (Table 1.3).

Hygiene factors, which relate to the work setting and not to the content of the work, include adequate wages, comfortable and safe working conditions, fair company policies, and job security. These factors do not necessarily motivate employees to excel, but their absence may be a potential source of dissatisfaction and high turnover. Employee safety and comfort are clearly hygiene factors.

保健因素
hygiene factors
aspects of Herzberg's theory of motivation that focus on the work setting and not the content of the work; these aspects include adequate wages, comfortable and safe working conditions, fair company policies, and job security

Many people feel that a good salary is one of the most important job factors, even more important than job security and the chance to use one's mind and abilities. Salary and security, two of the hygiene factors identified by Herzberg, make it possible for employees to satisfy the physiological and security needs identified by Maslow. However, the presence of hygiene factors is unlikely to motivate employees to work harder. For example, many people do not feel motivated to pursue a career as a gastroenterologist (doctors who specialize in the digestive system). Although the job is important and pays more than $250,000 on average, the tasks are routine and most patients are not looking forward to their appointments.[9]

TABLE 1.3
Herzberg's Hygiene and Motivational Factors

Hygiene Factors	Motivational Factors
Company policies	Achievement
Supervision	Recognition
Working conditions	Work itself
Relationships with peers, supervisors, and subordinates	Responsibility
Salary	Advancement
Security	Personal growth

* 注：有需要 Connect 等在线资源的读者请致电麦格劳－希尔教育集团北京办公室 010–57997618。

激励因素
motivational factors
aspects of Herzberg's theory of motivation that focus on the content of the work itself; these aspects include achievement, recognition, involvement, responsibility, and advancement

Motivational factors, which relate to the content of the work itself, include achievement, recognition, involvement, responsibility, and advancement. The absence of motivational factors may not result in dissatisfaction, but their presence is likely to motivate employees to excel. Many companies are beginning to employ methods to give employees more responsibility and control and to involve them more in their work, which serves to motivate them to higher levels of productivity and quality. Hotels are adopting more customer-centric processes in order to better their experiences. Doubletree, a franchise owned by Hilton Hotels and Resorts, has created a CARE committee for each of its locations. The committee is composed of employees from all departments so that they can ensure maximum operational performance and customer satisfaction. Marriott International employees leave personal notes for guests, and their loyalty program is above comparison.[10]

Herzberg's motivational factors and Maslow's esteem and self-actualization needs are similar. Workers' low-level needs (physiological and security) have largely been satisfied by minimum-wage laws and occupational-safety standards set by various government agencies and are therefore not motivators. Consequently, to improve productivity, management should focus on satisfying workers' higher-level needs (motivational factors) by providing opportunities for achievement, involvement, and advancement and by recognizing good performance.

麦格雷戈的 X 理论和 Y 理论
McGregor's Theory X and Theory Y

LO 1-4

In *The Human Side of Enterprise,* Douglas McGregor related Maslow's ideas about personal needs to management. McGregor contrasted two views of management—the traditional view, which he called Theory X, and a humanistic view, which he called Theory Y.

X 理论
Theory X
McGregor's traditional view of management whereby it is assumed that workers generally dislike work and must be forced to do their jobs

According to McGregor, managers adopting **Theory X** assume that workers generally dislike work and must be forced to do their jobs. They believe that the following statements are true of workers:

1. The average person naturally dislikes work and will avoid it when possible.
2. Most workers must be coerced, controlled, directed, or threatened with punishment to get them to work toward the achievement of organizational objectives.
3. The average worker prefers to be directed and to avoid responsibility, has relatively little ambition, and wants security.[11]

Managers who subscribe to the Theory X view maintain tight control over workers, provide almost constant supervision, try to motivate through fear, and make decisions in an autocratic fashion, eliciting little or no input from their subordinates. The Theory X style of management focuses on physiological and security needs and virtually ignores the higher needs discussed by Maslow. Foxconn, a manufacturing company that creates components for tech products such as the Apple iPad, is a company that had adopted the Theory X perspective.

Y 理论
Theory Y
McGregor's humanistic view of management whereby it is assumed that workers like to work and that under proper conditions employees will seek out responsibility in an attempt to satisfy their social, esteem, and self-actualization needs

The Theory X view of management does not take into account people's needs for companionship, esteem, and personal growth, whereas Theory Y, the contrasting view of management, does. Managers subscribing to the **Theory Y** view assume that workers like to work and that under proper conditions employees will seek out responsibility in an attempt to satisfy their social, esteem, and self-actualization needs. McGregor describes the assumptions behind Theory Y in the following way:

Entrepreneurship in Action

The Stein Mart Culture Is a Key Ingredient for Success

Stein Mart
Founder: Sam Stein
Founded: 1908, in Greenville, Mississippi
Success: Stein Mart has 263 retail stores in 29 states and earns more than $1 billion in total revenue.

Sam Stein couldn't have known that his small merchandise store in 1908 would one day grow into a thriving discount apparel chain helmed by his grandson. When Sam Stein's son took over, he shifted the emphasis to apparel and renamed the store. Today, grandson Jay Stein runs the company. While other regional, discount, and high-end retailers have struggled through the economic downturn, Stein Mart has maintained a strong presence in the market. Its competitive advantage is its pricing strategy—it offers quality goods at the prices of a discount retailer. Stein Mart does this by purchasing unsold merchandise from high-end retailers such as Saks Fifth Avenue and Neiman Marcus.

Stein's emphasis on customers and employees contributes to the personal culture of the company. Employees can receive health benefits, paid time off, and 25 percent discounts. Stein himself travels to stores weekly to meet and thank employees for their work. He also models good customer service by giving out thank-you notes to customers when they make purchases. These types of incentives add a personal touch absent from other retailers, resulting in high employee empowerment.[12]

---

1. The expenditure of physical and mental effort in work is as natural as play or rest.
2. People will exercise self-direction and self-control to achieve objectives to which they are committed.
3. People will commit to objectives when they realize that the achievement of those goals will bring them personal reward.
4. The average person will accept and seek responsibility.
5. Imagination, ingenuity, and creativity can help solve organizational problems, but most organizations do not make adequate use of these characteristics in their employees.
6. Organizations today do not make full use of workers' intellectual potential.[13]

Obviously, managers subscribing to the Theory Y philosophy have a management style very different from managers subscribing to the Theory X philosophy. Theory Y managers maintain less control and supervision, do not use fear as the primary motivator, and are more democratic in decision making, allowing subordinates to participate in the process. Theory Y managers address the high-level needs in Maslow's hierarchy as well as physiological and security needs. For instance, the Virgin Group, which is a conglomerate of various businesses in many industries, allows CEOs and managers to run their locations as they see fit. This also applies to complicated expansion measures such as opening foreign locations, which can become very complex. The company has achieved success by empowering employees to make their own decisions and follow their passions.[14] Today, Theory Y enjoys widespread support and may have displaced Theory X.

Z理论
Theory Z

Z理论
Theory Z
a management philosophy that stresses employee participation in all aspects of company decision making

Theory Z is a management philosophy that stresses employee participation in all aspects of company decision making. It was first described by William Ouchi in his book *Theory Z—How American Business Can Meet the Japanese Challenge.* Theory Z incorporates many elements associated with the Japanese approach to

TABLE 1.4 Comparison of American, Japanese, and Theory Z Management Styles

	American	Japanese	Theory Z
Duration of employment	Relatively short term; workers subject to layoffs when business slows	Lifelong; no layoffs	Long term; layoffs rare
Rate of promotion	Rapid	Slow	Slow
Amount of specialization	Considerable; worker develops expertise in one area only	Minimal; worker develops expertise in all aspects of the organization	Moderate; worker learns all aspects of the organization
Decision making	Individual	Consensual; input from all concerned parties is considered	Consensual; emphasis on quality
Responsibility	Assigned to the individual	Shared by the group	Assigned to the individual
Control	Explicit and formal	Less explicit and less formal	Informal but with explicit performance measures
Concern for workers	Focus is on work only	Focus extends to worker's whole life	Focus includes worker's life and family

Source: Adapted from William Ouchi, Theory Z—How American Business Can Meet the Japanese Challenge, *p. 58. © 1981 by Addison-Wesley Publishing Company, Inc.*

management, such as trust and intimacy, but Japanese ideas have been adapted for use in the United States. In a Theory Z organization, managers and workers share responsibilities; the management style is participative; and employment is long term and often lifelong. Japan has faced a significant period of slowing economic progress and competition from China and other Asian nations. This has led to experts questioning Theory Z, particularly at firms such as Sony and Toyota. Theory Z results in employees feeling organizational ownership. Research has found that such feelings of ownership may produce positive attitudinal and behavioral effects for employees.[15] In a Theory Y organization, managers focus on assumptions about the nature of the worker. The two theories can be seen as complementary. Table 1.4 compares the traditional American management style, the Japanese management style, and Theory Z (the modified Japanese management style).

公平理论
equity theory
an assumption that how much people are willing to contribute to an organization depends on their assessment of the fairness, or equity, of the rewards they will receive in exchange

公平理论
Equity Theory

According to **equity theory,** how much people are willing to contribute to an organization depends on their assessment of the fairness, or equity, of the rewards they will receive in exchange. In a fair situation, a person receives rewards proportional to the contribution he or she makes to the organization. However, in practice, equity is a subjective notion. Each worker regularly develops a personal input-output ratio by taking stock of his or her contribution (inputs) to the organization in time, effort, skills, and experience and assessing the rewards (outputs) offered by the organization in pay, benefits, recognition, and promotions. The worker compares his or her ratio to the input-output ratio of some other person—a "comparison other," who may be a co-worker, a friend working in another organization, or an "average" of several people working in the organization. If the two ratios are close, the individual will feel that he or she is being treated equitably.

Let's say you have a high-school education and earn $25,000 a year. When you compare your input-output ratio with that of a co-worker who has a college degree and makes $35,000 a year, you will probably feel that you are being paid fairly. However, if you perceive that your personal input-output ratio is lower than that of your college-educated co-worker, you may feel that you are being treated unfairly and be motivated to seek change. Or if you learn that your co-worker who makes $35,000 has only a high-school diploma, you may feel cheated by your employer. To achieve equity, you could try to increase your outputs by asking for a raise or promotion. You could also try to have your co-worker's inputs increased or his or her outputs decreased. Failing to achieve equity, you may be motivated to look for a job at a different company.

Equity theory might explain why many consumers are upset about CEO compensation. Although the job of the CEO can be incredibly stressful, the fact that they take home millions in compensation, bonuses, and stock options has been questioned. The high unemployment rate coupled with the misconduct that occurred at some large corporations prior to the recession contributed largely to the Occupy Wall Street protests. To counter this perception of pay inequality, several corporations have now begun to tie CEO compensation with company performance. If the company performs poorly for the year, then firms such as Goldman Sachs will cut bonuses and other compensation.[16] While lower compensation rates might appease the general public, some companies are worried that lower pay might deter talented individuals from wanting to assume the position of CEO at their firms.

Because almost all the issues involved in equity theory are subjective, they can be problematic. Author David Callahan has argued that feelings of inequity may underlie some unethical or illegal behavior in business. For example, due to employee theft and shoplifting, Walmart experiences billions in inventory losses every year. Some employees may take company resources to restore what they perceive to be equity. Theft of company resources is a major ethical issue, based on a survey by the Ethics Resource Center.[17] Callahan believes that employees who do not feel they are being treated equitably may be motivated to equalize the situation by lying, cheating, or otherwise "improving" their pay, perhaps by stealing.[18] Managers should try to avoid equity problems by ensuring that rewards are distributed on the basis of performance and that all employees clearly understand the basis for their pay and benefits.

期望理论
expectancy theory
the assumption that motivation depends not only on how much a person wants something but also on how likely he or she is to get it

期望理论

Expectancy Theory

Psychologist Victor Vroom described **expectancy theory,** which states that motivation depends not only on how much a person wants something but also on the person's perception of how likely he or she is to get it. A person who wants something and has reason to be optimistic will be strongly motivated. For example, say you really want a promotion. And let's say because you have taken some night classes to improve your skills, and moreover, have just made a large, significant sale, you feel confident that you are qualified and able to handle the new position. Therefore, you are motivated to try to get the promotion. In contrast, if you do not believe you are likely to get what you want, you may not be motivated to try to get it, even though you really want it.

Your motivation depends not only on how much you want something, but also on how likely you are to get it.

员工激励策略
Strategies for Motivating Employees

Based on the various theories that attempt to explain what motivates employees, businesses have developed several strategies for motivating their employees and boosting morale and productivity. Some of these techniques include behavior modification and job design, as well as the already described employee involvement programs and work teams.

行为塑造
Behavior Modification

LO 1-5

行为塑造
behavior modification
changing behavior and encouraging appropriate actions by relating the consequences of behavior to the behavior itself

Behavior modification involves changing behavior and encouraging appropriate actions by relating the consequences of behavior to the behavior itself. The concept of behavior modification was developed by psychologist B. F. Skinner, who showed that there are two types of consequences that can modify behavior—reward and punishment. Skinner found that behavior that is rewarded will tend to be repeated, while behavior that is punished will tend to be eliminated. For example, employees who know that they will receive a bonus such as an expensive restaurant meal for making a sale over $2,000 may be more motivated to make sales. Workers who know they will be punished for being tardy are likely to make a greater effort to get to work on time.

However, the two strategies may not be equally effective. Punishing unacceptable behavior may provide quick results but may lead to undesirable long-term side effects, such as employee dissatisfaction and increased turnover. In general, rewarding appropriate behavior is a more effective way to modify behavior.

工作设计
Job Design

Herzberg identified the job itself as a motivational factor. Managers have several strategies that they can use to design jobs to help improve employee motivation. These include job rotation, job enlargement, job enrichment, and flexible scheduling strategies.

岗位轮换
job rotation
movement of employees from one job to another in an effort to relieve the boredom often associated with job specialization

岗位轮换

Job Rotation. **Job rotation** allows employees to move from one job to another in an effort to relieve the boredom that is often associated with job specialization. Businesses often turn to specialization in hopes of increasing productivity, but there is a negative side effect to this type of job design: Employees become bored and dissatisfied, and productivity declines. Job rotation reduces this boredom by allowing workers to undertake a greater variety of tasks and by giving them the opportunity to learn new skills. With job rotation, an employee spends a specified amount of time performing one job and then moves on to another, different job. The worker eventually returns to the initial job and begins the cycle again.

Job rotation is a good idea, but it has one major drawback. Because employees may eventually become bored with all the jobs in the cycle, job rotation does not totally eliminate the problem of boredom. Job rotation is extremely useful, however, in situations where a person is being trained for a position that requires an understanding of various units in an organization. Eli Lilly is a strong believer in the benefits of job rotation. The company leaves employees in their current jobs and asks them to take on short-term assignments outside their field of expertise or interest. The results of the process have been positive, and Nokia is trying the same process with similar outcomes.[19] Many executive training programs require trainees to spend time learning a variety of specialized jobs. Job rotation is also used to cross-train today's self-directed work teams.

扩大职务

Job Enlargement. **Job enlargement** adds more tasks to a job instead of treating each task as separate. Like job rotation, job enlargement was developed to overcome the boredom associated with specialization. The rationale behind this strategy is that jobs are more satisfying as the number of tasks performed by an individual increases. Employees sometimes enlarge, or craft, their jobs by noticing what needs to be done and then changing tasks and relationship boundaries to adjust. Individual orientation and motivation shape opportunities to craft new jobs and job relationships. Job enlargement strategies have been more successful in increasing job satisfaction than have job rotation strategies. IBM, AT&T, and Maytag are among the many companies that have used job enlargement to motivate employees.

扩大职务
job enlargement
the addition of more tasks to a job instead of treating each task as separate

充实职务

Job Enrichment. **Job enrichment** incorporates motivational factors such as opportunity for achievement, recognition, responsibility, and advancement into a job. It gives workers not only more tasks within the job, but more control and authority over the job. Job enrichment programs enhance a worker's feeling of responsibility and provide opportunities for growth and advancement when the worker is able to take on the more challenging tasks. Hyatt Hotels Corporation and Clif Bar use job enrichment to improve the quality of work life for their employees. The potential benefits of job enrichment are great, but it requires careful planning and execution.

充实职务
job enrichment
the incorporation of motivational factors, such as opportunity for achievement, recognition, responsibility, and advancement, into a job

灵活工作制度策略

Flexible Scheduling Strategies. Many U.S. workers work a traditional 40-hour workweek consisting of five 8-hour days with fixed starting and ending times. Facing problems of poor morale and high absenteeism as well as a diverse workforce with changing needs, many managers have turned to flexible scheduling strategies such as flextime, compressed workweeks, job sharing, part-time work, and telecommuting. A survey by WorldatWork showed that 88 percent of businesses offer some sort of telecommuting work. Employees have shown greater commitment to these organizations, reducing turnover and increasing job satisfaction.[20]

Flextime is a program that allows employees to choose their starting and ending times, as long as they are at work during a specified core period (Figure 1.4). It does not reduce the total number of hours that employees work; instead, it gives employees more flexibility in choosing which hours they work. A firm may specify that employees must be present from 10:00 a.m. to 3:00 p.m. One employee may choose to come in at 7:00 a.m. and leave at the end of the core time, perhaps to attend classes at a nearby college after work. Another employee, a mother who lives in the suburbs, may

弹性工作制
flextime
a program that allows employees to choose their starting and ending times, provided that they are at work during a specified core period

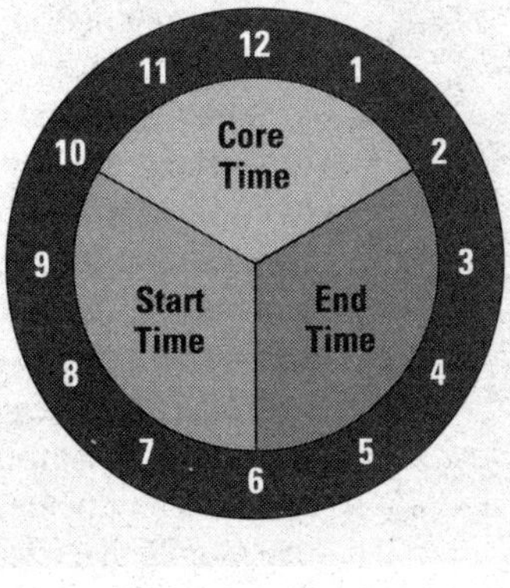

FIGURE 1.4
Flextime, Showing Core and Flexible Hours

come in at 9:00 a.m. in order to have time to drop off her children at a day-care center and commute by public transportation to her job. Flextime provides many benefits, including improved ability to recruit and retain workers who wish to balance work and home life. Customers can be better served by allowing more coverage of customers over longer hours, workstations and facilities can be better utilized by staggering employee use, and rush hour traffic may be reduced. In addition, flexible schedules have been associated with an increase in healthy behaviors on the part of employees. More flexible schedules are associated with healthier lifestyle choices such as increased physical activity and healthier sleep habits.[21]

压缩工作周
compressed workweek
a four-day (or shorter) period during which an employee works 40 hours

Related to flextime are the scheduling strategies of the compressed workweek and job sharing. The **compressed workweek** is a four-day (or shorter) period in which an employee works 40 hours. Under such a plan, employees typically work 10 hours per day for four days and have a three-day weekend. The compressed workweek reduces the company's operating expenses because its actual hours of operation are reduced. It is also sometimes used by parents who want to have more days off to spend with their families. The U.S. Bureau of Labor Statistics notes that the following career options provide greater flexibility in scheduling: medical transcriptionist, financial manager, nurse, database administrator, accountant, software developer, physical therapist assistant, paralegal, graphic designer, and private investigator.[22]

工作分担
job sharing
performance of one full-time job by two people on part-time hours

Job sharing occurs when two people do one job. One person may work from 8:00 a.m. to 12:30 p.m.; the second person comes in at 12:30 p.m. and works until 5:00 p.m. Job sharing gives both people the opportunity to work as well as time to fulfill other obligations, such as parenting or school. With job sharing, the company has the benefit of the skills of two people for one job, often at a lower total cost for salaries and benefits than one person working eight hours a day would be paid.

Two other flexible scheduling strategies attaining wider use include allowing full-time workers to work part time for a certain period and allowing workers to work at home either full or part time. Employees at some firms may be permitted to work part time for several months in order to care for a new baby or an elderly parent or just to slow down for a little while to "recharge their batteries." When the employees return to full-time work, they are usually given a position comparable to their original full-time position. Other firms are allowing employees to telecommute or telework (work at home a few days of the week), staying connected via computers, modems, and telephones. Most telecommuters tend to combine going into the office with working from home. Only about 3.3 million employees (not including entrepreneurs) cite the home as their primary workplace.[23]

Working from home is becoming increasingly common. Telecommuting, job sharing, and flextime can be beneficial for employees who cannot work normal work hours.

Although many employees ask for the option of working at home to ease the responsibilities of caring for family members, some have discovered that they are more productive at home without the distractions of the workplace. PGi conducted a survey on telecommuting and found that telecommuters experienced a decrease in stress and absenteeism and an increase in morale and productivity. Perhaps due to the positive morale that telecommuting can create, many

Responding to Business Challenges

The Pros and Cons of Working from Home

Allowing employees to work from home, known as telecommuting, has become a controversial topic for managers and human resources departments. With the advancement of technology, telecommuting has become easier and a part of many companies' cultures. It has been reported that 80 percent of companies listed on *Fortune*'s "Best Companies to Work For" offer employees the opportunity to work from home. Telecommuting has become a major benefit for employees. However, working from home has many challenges, and some firms are reversing their companies' work-from-home policies. Yahoo! CEO Marissa Mayer declared that the majority of Yahoo! employees would no longer be allowed to work from home because she believes employees need to interact with one another to improve productivity and cohesiveness. Bank of America and Best Buy have also reduced or eliminated work-from-home programs.

For many employees, working from home provides the benefit of achieving a work/life balance. Studies have shown that working from home can provide a happier environment and foster stronger loyalty from employees. This idea can be used as a motivational tool for employees if proper communication is provided linking employees to their businesses.

However, some employers believe that telecommuting is allowing collaboration among employees to suffer. By working from home, employees are becoming independent and potentially isolated, creating disconnections within the company. Also, employers are questioning whether employees abuse this privilege and are less efficient than they would be in an office environment. The question of whether telecommuting is productive and beneficial for the company remains a center of debate.[24]

Discussion Questions

1. What are the advantages of using work-from-home policies to motivate employees?
2. What are the disadvantages of using work-from-home policies to motivate employees?
3. What impact do you feel reversing a firm's work-from-home policies will have on employee motivation?

Fortune 500 companies—including Apple, Google, and J. P. Morgan Chase—offer several types of telecommuting positions.[25] Other employees, however, have discovered that they are not suited for working at home. For telecommuting to work, it must be a feasible alternative and must not create significant costs for the company.[26] Bank of America, Yahoo!, and Best Buy are all eliminating their work-from-home programs as they feel that being present in the workplace increases collaboration and productivity. Still, work-at-home programs can help reduce overhead costs for businesses. For example, some companies used to maintain a surplus of office space but have reduced the surplus through employee telecommuting, "hoteling" (being assigned to a desk through a reservation system), and "hot-desking" (several people using the same desk but at different times).

Companies are turning to flexible work schedules to provide more options to employees who are trying to juggle their work duties with other responsibilities and needs. Preliminary results indicate that flexible scheduling plans increase job satisfaction, which, in turn, leads to increases in productivity. Some recent research, however, has indicated there are potential problems with telecommuting. Some managers are reluctant to adopt the practice because the pace of change in today's workplace is faster than ever, and telecommuters may be left behind or actually cause managers more work in helping them stay abreast of changes. Some employers also worry that telecommuting workers create a security risk by creating more opportunities for computer hackers or equipment thieves. Some employees have found that working outside the office may hurt career advancement opportunities, and some report that instead of helping them balance work and family responsibilities, telecommuting increases the strain by blurring the barriers between the office and home. Co-workers call at all

Businesses have come up with different ways to motivate employees, including rewards such as trophies and plaques to show the company's appreciation.

hours, and telecommuters are apt to continue to work when they are not supposed to (after regular business hours or during vacation time).

激励策略的重要性 Importance of Motivational Strategies

Motivation is more than a tool that managers can use to foster employee loyalty and boost productivity. It is a process that affects all the relationships within an organization and influences many areas such as pay, promotion, job design, training opportunities, and reporting relationships. Employees are motivated by the nature of the relationships they have with their supervisors, by the nature of their jobs, and by characteristics of the organization. Table 1.5 shows companies with excellent motivational strategies, along with the types of strategies they use to motivate employees. Even the economic environment can change an employee's motivation. In a slow growth or recession economy, sales can flatten or decrease and morale can drop because of the need to cut jobs. In the most recent recession, many workers feared losing their jobs and increased the amount they were

TABLE 1.5 Companies with Excellent Motivational Strategies

Company	Motivational Strategies
3M	Gives employees 15–20 percent of their time to pursue on projects
Google	Perks include a massage every other week, free gourmet lunches, tuition reimbursement, a volleyball court, and time to work on own projects
Whole Foods	Employees receive 20 percent discounts on company products, the opportunity to gain stock options, and the ability to make major decisions in small teams
Patagonia	Provides areas for yoga and aerobics, in-house child care services, organic food in its café, and opportunities to go surfing during the day
The Container Store	Provides more than 260 hours of employee training and hosts "We Love Our Employees" Day
Southwest Airlines	Gives employees permission to interact with passengers as they see fit, provides free or discounted flights, and hosts the "Adopt-a-Pilot" program to connect pilots with students across the nation
Nike	Offers tuition assistance, product discounts, onsite fitness centers, and the ability for employees to give insights on how to improve the firm
Apple	Creates a fast-paced, innovative work environment where employees are encouraged to debate ideas
Marriott	Offers discounts at hotels across the world as well as free hotel stays and travel opportunities for employees with exceptional service
Zappos	Creates a fun, zany work environment for employees and empowers them to take as much times as needed to answer customer concerns

saving. The firm may have to work harder to keep good employees and to motivate all employees to work to overcome obstacles. In good economic times, employees may be more demanding and be on the lookout for better opportunities. New rewards or incentives may help motivate workers in such economies. Motivation tools, then, must be varied as well. Managers can further nurture motivation by being honest, supportive, empathic, accessible, fair, and open. Motivating employees to increase satisfaction and productivity is an important concern for organizations seeking to remain competitive in the global marketplace.

So You Think You May Be Good at Motivating a Workforce

If you are good at mediation, smoothing conflict, and have a good understanding of motivation and human relations theories, then you might be a good leader, human resource manager, or training expert. Most organizations, especially as they grow, will need to implement human relations programs. These are necessary to teach employees about sensitivity to other cultures, religions, and beliefs, as well as for teaching the workforce about the organization so that they understand how they fit in the larger picture. Employees need to appreciate the benefits of working together to make the firm run smoothly, and they also need to understand how their contributions help the firm. To stay motivated, most employees need to feel like what they do each day contributes something of value to the firm. Disclosing information and including employees in decision-making processes will also help employees feel valuable and wanted within the firm.

There are many different ways employers can reward and encourage employees. However, employers must be careful when considering what kinds of incentives to use. Different cultures value different kinds of incentives more highly than others. For example, a Japanese worker would probably not like it if she were singled out from the group and given a large cash bonus as reward for her work. Japanese workers tend to be more group oriented, and therefore anything that singles out individuals would not be an effective way of rewarding and motivating. American workers, on the other hand, are very individualistic, and a raise and public praise might be more effective. However, what might motivate a younger employee (bonuses, raises, and perks) may not be the same as what motivates a more seasoned, experienced, and financially successful employee (recognition, opportunity for greater influence, and increased training). Motivation is not an easy thing to understand, especially as firms become more global and more diverse.

Another important part of motivation is enjoying where you work and your career opportunities. Here is a list of the best places to do business and start careers in the United States, according to *Forbes* magazine. Chances are, workers who live in these places have encountered fewer frustrations than those places at the bottom of the list and, therefore, would probably be more content with where they work.[27]

Best Places for Businesses and Careers[28]

Rank	Metro Area	Gross Metro Product*	Metro Population
1.	Des Moines, Iowa	$37 billion	589,500
2.	Provo, Utah	$18 billion	552,800
3.	Raleigh, North Carolina	$58 billion	1,194,100
4.	Lincoln, Nebraska	$17 billion	310,700
5.	Nashville, Tennessee	$83 billion	1,647,200
6.	Denver, Colorado	$153 billion	2,649,400
7.	Fort Collins, Colorado	$15 billion	311,300
8.	Oklahoma City, Oklahoma	$59 billion	1,297,900
9.	Seattle, Washington	$203 billion	2,744,100
10.	Durham, North Carolina	$34 billion	523,600

**Gross metro product is the market value of all products produced within a metropolitan area in a given time period; similar to GDP but on a metropolitan area.*

Review Your Understanding

Define human relations, and determine why its study is important.

Human relations is the study of the behavior of individuals and groups in organizational settings. Its focus is what motivates employees to perform on the job. Human relations is important because businesses need to understand how to motivate their increasingly diverse employees to be more effective, boost workplace morale, and maximize employees' productivity and creativity.

Summarize studies that laid the groundwork for understanding employee motivation.

Time and motion studies by Frederick Taylor and others helped them analyze how employees perform specific work tasks in an effort to improve their productivity. Taylor and the early practitioners of the classical theory of motivation felt that money and job security were the primary motivators of employees. However, the Hawthorne studies revealed that human factors also influence workers' behavior.

Compare and contrast the human-relations theories of Abraham Maslow and Frederick Herzberg.

Abraham Maslow defined five basic needs of all people and arranged them in the order in which they must be satisfied: physiological, security, social, esteem, and self-actualization. Frederick Herzberg divided characteristics of the job into hygiene factors and motivational factors. Hygiene factors relate to the work environment and must be present for employees to remain in a job. Motivational factors—recognition, responsibility, and advancement—relate to the work itself. They encourage employees to be productive. Herzberg's hygiene factors can be compared to Maslow's physiological and security needs; motivational factors may include Maslow's social, esteem, and self-actualization needs.

Investigate various theories of motivation, including theories X, Y, and Z; equity theory; and expectancy theory.

Douglas McGregor contrasted two views of management: Theory X (traditional) suggests workers dislike work, while theory Y (humanistic) suggests that workers not only like work but seek out responsibility to satisfy their higher-order needs. Theory Z stresses employee participation in all aspects of company decision making, often through participative management programs and self-directed work teams. According to equity theory, how much people are willing to contribute to an organization depends on their assessment of the fairness, or equity, of the rewards they will receive in exchange. Expectancy theory states that motivation depends not only on how much a person wants something but also on the person's perception of how likely he or she is to get it.

Describe some of the strategies that managers use to motivate employees.

Strategies for motivating workers include behavior modification (changing behavior and encouraging appropriate actions by relating the consequences of behavior to the behavior itself) and job design. Among the job design strategies businesses use are job rotation (allowing employees to move from one job to another to try to relieve the boredom associated with job specialization), job enlargement (adding tasks to a job instead of treating each task as a separate job), job enrichment (incorporating motivational factors into a job situation), and flexible scheduling strategies (flextime, compressed workweeks, job sharing, part-time work, and telecommuting).

Critique a business's program for motivating its sales force.

Using the information presented in the chapter, you should be able to analyze and defend Eagle Pharmaceutical's motivation program in "Solve the Dilemma" on page 284, including the motivation theories the firm is applying to boost morale and productivity.

Revisit the World of Business

1. Why do you think that Mars Inc. refuses to become a public company?
2. How does Mars Inc. motivate its employees?
3. How does employee motivation at Mars Inc. contribute to the firm's success?

Learn the Terms

behavior modification
classical theory of motivation
compressed workweek
equity theory
esteem needs
expectancy theory
extrinsic rewards
flextime
human relations
hygiene factors
intrinsic rewards
job enlargement
job enrichment
job rotation
job sharing
Maslow's hierarchy
morale
motivation
motivational factors
physiological needs
security needs

self-actualization needs
social needs
Theory X
Theory Y
Theory Z

Check Your Progress

1. Why do managers need to understand the needs of their employees?
2. Describe the motivation process.
3. What was the goal of the Hawthorne studies? What was the outcome of those studies?
4. Explain Maslow's hierarchy of needs. What does it tell us about employee motivation?
5. What are Herzberg's hygiene and motivational factors? How can managers use them to motivate workers?
6. Contrast the assumptions of theory X and theory Y. Why has theory Y replaced theory X in management today?
7. What is theory Z? How can businesses apply theory Z to the workplace?
8. Identify and describe four job-design strategies.
9. Name and describe some flexible scheduling strategies. How can flexible schedules help motivate workers?
10. Why are motivational strategies important to both employees and employers?

Get Involved

1. Consider a person who is homeless: How would he or she be motivated and what actions would that person take? Use the motivation process to explain. Which of the needs in Maslow's hierarchy are likely to be most important? Least important?
2. View the video *Cheaper by the Dozen* (1950) and report on how the Gilbreths tried to incorporate their passion for efficiency into their family life.
3. What events and trends in society, technology, and economics do you think will shape human relations management theory in the future?

Build Your Skills

Motivating

Background

Do you think that, if employers could make work more like play, employees would be as enthusiastic about their jobs as they are about what they do in their leisure time? Let's see where this idea might take us.

Task

After reading the "Characteristics of PLAY," place a √ in column one for those characteristics you have experienced in your leisure time activities. Likewise, check column three for those "Characteristics of WORK" you have experienced in any of the jobs you've held.

All That Apply	Characteristics of PLAY	All That Apply	Characteristics of WORK
	1. New games can be played on different days.		1. Job enrichment, job enlargement, or job rotation.
	2. Flexible duration of play.		2. Job sharing.
	3. Flexible time of when to play.		3. Flextime, telecommuting.
	4. Opportunity to express oneself.		4. Encourage and implement employee suggestions.
	5. Opportunity to use one's talents.		5. Assignment of challenging projects.
	6. Skillful play brings applause, praise, and recognition from spectators.		6. Employee-of-the-month awards, press releases, employee newsletter announcements.
	7. Healthy competition, rivalry, and challenge exist.		7. Production goals with competition to see which team does best.
	8. Opportunity for social interaction.		8. Employee softball or bowling teams.
	9. Mechanisms for scoring one's performance are available (feedback).		9. Profit sharing; peer performance appraisals.
	10. Rules ensure basic fairness and justice.		10. Use tactful and consistent discipline.

Discussion Questions

1. What prevents managers from making work more like play?
2. Are these forces real or imagined?
3. What would be the likely (positive and negative) results of making work more like play?
4. Could others in the organization accept such creative behaviors?

Solve the Dilemma LO 1-6

Motivating to Win

Eagle Pharmaceutical has long been recognized for its innovative techniques for motivating its salesforce. It features the salesperson who has been the most successful during the previous quarter in the company newsletter, "Touchdown." The salesperson also receives a football jersey, a plaque, and $1,000 worth of Eagle stock. Eagle's "Superbowl Club" is for employees who reach or exceed their sales goal, and a "Heisman Award," which includes a trip to the Caribbean, is given annually to the top 20 salespeople in terms of goal achievement.

Eagle employs a video conference hookup between the honored salesperson and four regional sales managers to capture some of the successful tactics and strategies the winning salesperson uses to succeed. The managers summarize these ideas and pass them along to the salespeople they manage. Sales managers feel strongly that programs such as this are important and that, by sharing strategies and tactics with one another, they can be a successful team.

Discussion Questions

1. Which motivational theories are in use at Eagle?
2. What is the value of getting employees to compete against a goal instead of against one another?
3. Put yourself in the shoes of one of the four regional sales managers and argue against potential cutbacks to the motivational program.

Build Your Business Plan

Motivating the Workforce

As you determine the size of your workforce, you are going to face the reality that you cannot provide the level of financial compensation that you would like to your employees, especially when you are starting your business.

Many employees are motivated by other things than money. Knowing that they are appreciated and doing a good job can bring great satisfaction to employees. Known as "stroking," it can provide employees with internal gratification that can be valued even more than financial incentives. Listening to your employees' suggestions, involving them in discussions about future growth, and valuing their input can go a long way toward building loyal employees and reducing employee turnover.

Think about what you could do in your business to motivate your employees without spending much money. Maybe you will have lunch brought in once a week or offer tickets to a local sporting event to the employee with the most sales. Whatever you elect to do, you must be consistent and fair with all your employees.

See for Yourself Videocase

The Container Store's Secret to Success: Employee Satisfaction

Can you form a successful company by selling containers, boxes, and other storage products? The Container Store has shown that the answer is yes. With more than 10,000 products available, The Container Store sells items such as hanging bins, drawers, trash cans, and other items to help make a hectic life more organized. While there might have been skeptics in the beginning, particularly as the firm started out in a small 1,600 square-foot store, the idea quickly caught on with consumers.

"Word of mouth spread incredibly. It was just the oddest collection of merchandising anybody had ever seen to organize your home and to organize your life. A week into it, we knew we had something," co-founder and CEO Kip Tindell said.

Yet in addition to its unusual product mix, The Container Store is also unique for its dedication to employees. The retail world can be difficult for employees because of high turnover, different hours every week, lower benefits, and constant interaction with people. The turnover rate in the retail industry is about 100 percent. This increases training costs, which can cause companies to decrease the amount of training offered.

This trend is reversed at The Container Store. First-year full-time employees receive 263 hours of training, much higher than the industry average of 10 hours. Employees receive 50 percent more pay than at other retail establishments. Employee turnover at The Container Store is a low 10 percent. For more than a decade, The Container Store has been elected as one of the top 100 companies to work for by *Fortune* magazine.

Yet, the satisfaction that employees feel toward the company is not solely a result of higher pay. According to Frederick Herzberg's two-factor theory, good workplace conditions can prevent dissatisfaction but do not motivate the employee to go above and beyond what is required of them. As CEO of the company, Kip Tindell realizes that the amount of time and effort an employee gives to the company will determine productivity.

"The first 25 percent for any employee is mandatory. If they don't do that, they're going to get fired. But the next 75 percent of an employee's productivity for any business in the world, I believe, is more or less voluntary. You do more or less of it depending upon how you feel about your boss and your product and your company."

Therefore, to enhance productivity, the firm has made employee satisfaction a priority. Employees come first, followed by customers and then shareholders. One of the ways that The Container Store motivates its employees is by creating an open communication culture. Employees are encouraged to approach their managers on any topic. This causes employees to feel as if the organization cares about them enough to take their concerns seriously. The Container Store also holds several events to show their appreciation of employee efforts. For instance, every February 14, The Container Store holds its "We Love Our Employees" day. At one of the events, the company announced the establishment of an emergency fund for employees. The company contributed $100,000 for unexpected costs that employees may find themselves having to pay for due to natural disasters, terrorist attacks, or significant medical issues.

Employees also receive many perks for working at The Container Store, and even part-time employees are eligible for health care benefits. Because employees take precedence at The Container Store, the company bases its decisions on what is best for employees even during hard times. During the recession, for instance, The Container Store refused to lay off employees. In addition to benefits, employees have access to all company data, including financial reports.

Does this mean that The Container Store ignores its customers for the sake of its employees? The high-quality customer service that The Container Store offers suggests just the opposite. In fact, the extensive employee training and the company's values demonstrate its high commitment to customer satisfaction. According to Tindell, the key to great customer service, however, is highly motivated employees.

"We believe that if you take better care of your employees than anybody else, they'll take better care of the customer than anybody else, and if those two guys are ecstatic, ironically enough, your shareholder's going to be ecstatic too."[29]

Discussion Questions

1. Name some of the hygiene factors at The Container Store.
2. Name some of the ways that The Container Store motivates its employees.
3. Do you believe Tindell's statement that highly satisfied employees will lead to highly satisfied customers and shareholders?

You can find the related video in the Video Library in Connect. Ask your instructor how you can access Connect.

Team Exercise

Form groups and outline a compensation package that you would consider ideal in motivating an employee, recognizing performance, and assisting the company in attaining its cost-to-performance objectives. Think about the impact of intrinsic and extrinsic motivation and recognition. How can flexible scheduling strategies be used effectively to motivate employees? Report your compensation package to the class.

2

Organization, Teamwork, and Communication

组织、团队和沟通

Learning Objectives

After reading this chapter, you will be able to:

- **LO 2-1** Define organizational structure, and relate how organizational structures develop.
- **LO 2-2** Describe how specialization and departmentalization help an organization achieve its goals.
- **LO 2-3** Determine how organizations assign responsibility for tasks and delegate authority.
- **LO 2-4** Compare and contrast some common forms of organizational structure.
- **LO 2-5** Distinguish between groups and teams, and identify the types of groups that exist in organizations.
- **LO 2-6** Describe how communication occurs in organizations.
- **LO 2-7** Analyze a business's use of teams.

Chapter Outline

Introduction
Organizational Culture
Developing Organizational Structure
Assigning Tasks
 Specialization
 Departmentalization
Assigning Responsibility
 Delegation of Authority
 Degree of Centralization
 Span of Management
 Organizational Layers
Forms of Organizational Structure
 Line Structure
 Line-and-Staff Structure
 Multidivisional Structure
 Matrix Structure
The Role of Groups and Teams in Organizations
 Committees
 Task Forces
 Teams
Communicating in Organizations
 Formal Communication
 Informal Communication Channels
 Monitoring Communications
 Improving Communication Effectiveness

进入商业世界

Enter the World of Business

车美仕采用分权式组织结构加强团队合作

CarMax Uses Decentralized Structure to Support Teamwork

In 1991, some executives from Circuit City decided to test-launch a new business idea for a used car company termed Project X. Two years later, CarMax was officially launched. CarMax makes it a priority to develop satisfied employees. The company has a decentralized structure where employees are encouraged to submit recommendations and develop leadership skills. Over the past 20 years, CarMax has grown to 119 stores with 18,000 employees. In 2013, CarMax was listed as one of *Fortune's* Best Companies to Work For.

CarMax uses RFID technology to track how long cars sit in the lot, extensive sales data to determine inventory needs accurately, and a flat commission compensation system so salespeople will promote the cars that best meet customer needs rather than trying to sell the most expensive car.

Tom Folliard, the CEO of CarMax, learned that developing a decentralized corporate culture focusing on teamwork and employee empowerment generates positive results. CarMax prides itself on being founded on fundamental principles that every store must abide by. Values include respect, communication, customer focus, and teamwork. CarMax believes that employees who work together are able to place the customer first and serve their best interests. Folliard stays accessible for employees through town hall meetings and steak cookouts.

With this type of company culture, employees are able to feel a sense of ownership and high levels of contribution to the company. This allows for employees to hold themselves to higher standards, resulting in higher work performance. In an industry that has a certain stigma about car salespeople, CarMax's focus of empowering employees to provide quality customer service and take ownership of the company has revolutionized the used car industry.[1]

引言
Introduction

An organization's structure determines how well it makes decisions and responds to problems, and it influences employees' attitudes toward their work. A suitable structure can minimize a business's costs and maximize its efficiency. Even companies that operate within the same industry may utilize different organizational structures. For example, in the consumer electronics industry, Samsung is organized as a conglomerate with separate business units or divisions. Samsung is largely decentralized. Apple, under CEO Tim Cook, has moved from a hierarchical structure to a more collaborative approach between divisions.[2]

Because a business's structure can so profoundly affect its success, this chapter will examine organizational structure in detail. First, we discuss how an organization's culture affects its operations. Then we consider the development of structure, including how tasks and responsibilities are organized through specialization and departmentalization. Next, we explore some of the forms organizational structure may take. Finally, we consider communications within business.

组织文化
Organizational Culture

组织文化
organizational culture
a firm's shared values, beliefs, traditions, philosophies, rules, and role models for behavior

One of the most important aspects of organizing a business is determining its **organizational culture,** a firm's shared values, beliefs, traditions, philosophies, rules, and role models for behavior. Also called corporate culture, an organizational culture exists in every organization, regardless of size, organizational type, product, or profit objective. Sometimes behaviors, programs, and policies enhance and support the organizational culture. Netflix, for example, established a "freedom and responsibility culture," which has become a culture code many Silicon Valley companies have used as a template for establishing their organizational cultures. One way Netflix expresses this culture is by not having a vacation policy. Employees are expected to be responsible and disciplined while working, and in exchange, they are allowed the freedom to take vacation when they like and for as long as they like.[3] A firm's culture may be expressed formally through its mission statement, codes of ethics, memos, manuals, and ceremonies, but it is more commonly expressed informally. Examples of informal expressions of culture include dress codes (or the lack thereof), work habits, extracurricular activities, and stories. Employees often learn the accepted standards through discussions with co-workers.

TOMS Shoes' organizational culture is determined by the founder's desire to provide as many shoes as possible to children in developing countries (where shoeless children walk for miles to get water, food, and medical care). Blake Mycoskie gives hundreds of thousands of shoes to children around the world each year, creating a strong organizational culture of giving back and corporate social responsibility. His company operates with a program that for every pair of shoes purchased, a pair will be donated to children in need.[4] Disneyland/DisneyWorld and McDonald's have organizational cultures focused on cleanliness, value, and service. The company Zappos.com created a culture of "fun and a little weirdness." The company has a flexible work environment with very few rules, and employees are encouraged to socialize and engage in unique activities (such as ringing cowbells when visitors arrive). Zappos' goal is to make both employees and customers feel good. Customer service is such a must at Zappos that new hires must work for one month at a call center, even if the new employees are not going to be interacting with customers normally.[5] When such values

Responding to Business Challenges

Companies Embracing Greater Employee Interaction

Getting rid of cubicles, creating inconvenient work spaces, and eliminating work-from-home programs are some of the methods being used by companies to increase collaboration, communication, and teamwork. Yahoo! and Best Buy, for example, have eliminated their work-from-home programs to increase face-to-face interaction among employees. Studies have shown that employee interaction leads to more innovative ideas.

Google and Zappos are among those companies taking the lead in using their space to encourage collaboration and innovation. Both are designing new buildings with smaller workspaces and break rooms and narrower hallways so employees will see each other more often and have more opportunity for chance discussions. Zappos CEO Tony Hsieh is purposefully designing inconvenience into the new Zappos headquarters so that employees will have to interact with one another. Campbell's Soup is removing cubicles and installing more common spaces to increase employee teamwork and problem-solving.

Other companies are installing interactive devices in elevators where silence is usually the norm. Salesforce.com is installing a lunch button kiosk. Employees can push a button on the kiosk, and the kiosk matches a fellow co-worker that shares a common interest with the employee. The employee can then invite that person to lunch—and a new relationship is formed. This increase in interaction is anticipated to improve communication and relationships in companies.[6]

Discussion Questions

1. Describe methods some companies are using to increase employee interaction.
2. Why is it important that employees interact with one another?
3. Do you feel that the disadvantages of work-from-home programs are higher than their benefits?

and philosophies are shared by all members of an organization, they will be expressed in its relationships with stakeholders. However, organizational cultures that lack such positive values may result in employees who are unproductive and indifferent and have poor attitudes, which will be reflected externally to customers. The corporate culture may have contributed to the misconduct at a number of well-known companies. A survey found that executives in financial and technology companies are mostly cut-throat in collecting intelligence about competition, creating a corporate culture in which unethical acts might be tolerated if it means beating the competition.[7]

Organizational culture helps ensure that all members of a company share values and suggests rules for how to behave and deal with problems within the organization. Table 2.1 confirms that executives in this study believe that corporate culture has a significant impact on organizational performance and the ability to retain good employees. The key to success in any organization is satisfying stakeholders, especially customers. Establishing a positive organizational culture sets the tone for all other decisions, including building an efficient organizational structure.

The organizational structure at TOMS Shoes consists of two parts. The for-profit component of the company manages overall operations. Its nonprofit component, Friends of TOMS, is responsible for volunteer activities and shoe donations.

TABLE 2.1
Attitudes and Behaviors Associated with Corporate Cultures

	Employees Who View Their Culture Negatively	Employees Who View Their Culture Positively
Committed toward organization	17%	86%
Satisfied with organization	13	87
Likely to recommend their organization to others	13	88
Intend to leave the organizations	63	10
Alignment with leadership	8	59

N = 236 management and human resources professionals from U.S. companies with more than 100 employees.

Source: Survey conducted by Critical Metrics LLC, CR Magazine *3, June 2012.*

LO 2-1

结构
structure
the arrangement or relationship of positions within an organization

组织结构图
organizational chart
a visual display of the organizational structure, lines of authority (chain of command), staff relationships, permanent committee arrangements, and lines of communication

制定组织结构
Developing Organizational Structure

Structure is the arrangement or relationship of positions within an organization. Rarely is an organization, or any group of individuals working together, able to achieve common objectives without some form of structure, whether that structure is explicitly defined or only implied. A professional baseball team such as the Colorado Rockies is a business organization with an explicit formal structure that guides the team's activities so that it can increase game attendance, win games, and sell souvenirs such as T-shirts. But even an informal group playing softball for fun has an organization that specifies who will pitch, catch, bat, coach, and so on. Governments and nonprofit organizations also have formal organizational structures to facilitate the achievement of their objectives. Getting people to work together efficiently and coordinating the skills of diverse individuals require careful planning. Developing appropriate organizational structures is therefore a major challenge for managers in both large and small organizations.

An organization's structure develops when managers assign work tasks and activities to specific individuals or work groups and coordinate the diverse activities required to reach the firm's objectives. When Macy's, for example, has a sale, the store manager must work with the advertising department to make the public aware of the sale, with department managers to ensure that extra salespeople are scheduled to handle the increased customer traffic, and with merchandise buyers to ensure that enough sale merchandise is available to meet expected consumer demand. All the people occupying these positions must work together to achieve the store's objectives.

The best way to begin to understand how organizational structure develops is to consider the evolution of a new business such as a clothing store. At first, the business is a sole proprietorship in which the owner does everything—buys, prices, and displays the merchandise; does the accounting and tax records; and assists customers. As the business grows, the owner hires a salesperson and perhaps a merchandise buyer to help run the store. As the business continues to grow, the owner hires more salespeople. The growth and success of the business now require the owner to be away from the store frequently, meeting with suppliers, engaging in public relations, and attending trade shows. Thus, the owner must designate someone to manage the salespeople and maintain the accounting, payroll, and tax functions. If the owner decides to expand by opening more stores, still more managers will be needed. Figure 2.1 shows these stages of growth with three **organizational charts** (visual displays of organizational structure, chain of command, and other relationships).

FIGURE 2.1 The Evolution of a Clothing Store, Phases 1, 2, and 3

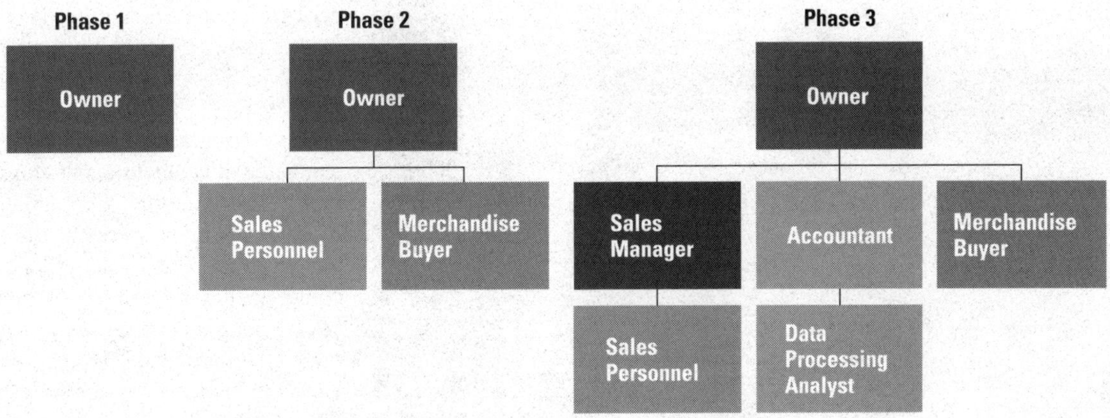

Growth requires organizing—the structuring of human, physical, and financial resources to achieve objectives in an effective and efficient manner. Growth necessitates hiring people who have specialized skills. With more people and greater specialization, the organization needs to develop a formal structure to function efficiently. Imagine the various organizational changes that Nokia has undergone. It was founded in 1865 as a paper mill in Finland and has become a global telecommunications company serving more than 1 billion customers. During its history, the company has transformed itself various times—including as a rubber company, television maker, and a cable company—each time changing the organizational structure to accommodate its business.[8] As we shall see, structuring an organization requires that management assign work tasks to specific individuals and departments and assign responsibility for the achievement of specific organizational objectives.

任务的分配
Assigning Tasks

LO 2-2

For a business to earn profits from the sale of its products, its managers must first determine what activities are required to achieve its objectives. At Celestial Seasonings, for example, employees must purchase herbs from suppliers, dry the herbs and place them in tea bags, package and label the tea, and then ship the packages to grocery stores around the country. Other necessary activities include negotiating with supermarkets and other retailers for display space, developing new products, planning advertising, managing finances, and managing employees. All these activities must be coordinated, assigned to work groups, and controlled. Two important aspects of assigning these work activities are specialization and departmentalization.

专业化
Specialization

After identifying all activities that must be accomplished, managers then break these activities down into specific tasks that can be handled by individual employees. This division of labor into small, specific tasks and the assignment of employees to do a single task is called **specialization.**

专业化
specialization
the division of labor into small, specific tasks and the assignment of employees to do a single task

Job specialization is common in automobile manufacturing. By dividing work into smaller specialized tasks, employees can perform their work more quickly and efficiently.

The rationale for specialization is efficiency. People can perform more efficiently if they master just one task rather than all tasks. In *The Wealth of Nations,* 18th-century economist Adam Smith discussed specialization, using the manufacture of straight pins as an example. Individually, workers could produce 20 pins a day when each employee produced complete pins. Thus, 10 employees working independently of each other could produce 200 pins a day. However, when one worker drew the wire, another straightened it, a third cut it, and a fourth ground the point, 10 workers could produce 48,000 pins per day.[9] To save money and achieve the benefits of specialization, some companies outsource and hire temporary workers to provide key skills. Many highly skilled, diverse, experienced workers are available through temp agencies.

Specialization means workers do not waste time shifting from one job to another, and training is easier. However, efficiency is not the only motivation for specialization. Specialization also occurs when the activities that must be performed within an organization are too numerous for one person to handle. Recall the example of the clothing store. When the business was young and small, the owner could do everything; but when the business grew, the owner needed help waiting on customers, keeping the books, and managing other business activities.

Overspecialization can have negative consequences. Employees may become bored and dissatisfied with their jobs, and the result of their unhappiness is likely to be poor quality work, more injuries, and high employee turnover. In extreme cases, employees in crowded specialized electronic plants are unable to form working relationships with one another. At Foxconn, a multinational electronics manufacturing firm and one of the suppliers of Apple iPhones and iPads, lack of working relationships, long work hours, low pay, and other conditions resulted in employee dissatisfaction and, tragically, depression and even suicide.[10] This is why some manufacturing firms allow job rotation so that employees do not become dissatisfied and leave. Although some degree of specialization is necessary for efficiency, because of differences in skills, abilities, and interests, all people are not equally suited for all jobs. We examine some strategies to overcome these issues in Chapter 1.

部门化
Departmentalization

部门化

departmentalization
the grouping of jobs into working units usually called departments, units, groups, or divisions

After assigning specialized tasks to individuals, managers next organize workers doing similar jobs into groups to make them easier to manage. **Departmentalization** is the grouping of jobs into working units usually called departments, units, groups, or divisions. As we shall see, departments are commonly organized by function, product, geographic region, or customer (Figure 2.2). Most companies use more than one departmentalization plan to enhance productivity. For instance, many consumer

FIGURE 2.2 Departmentalization

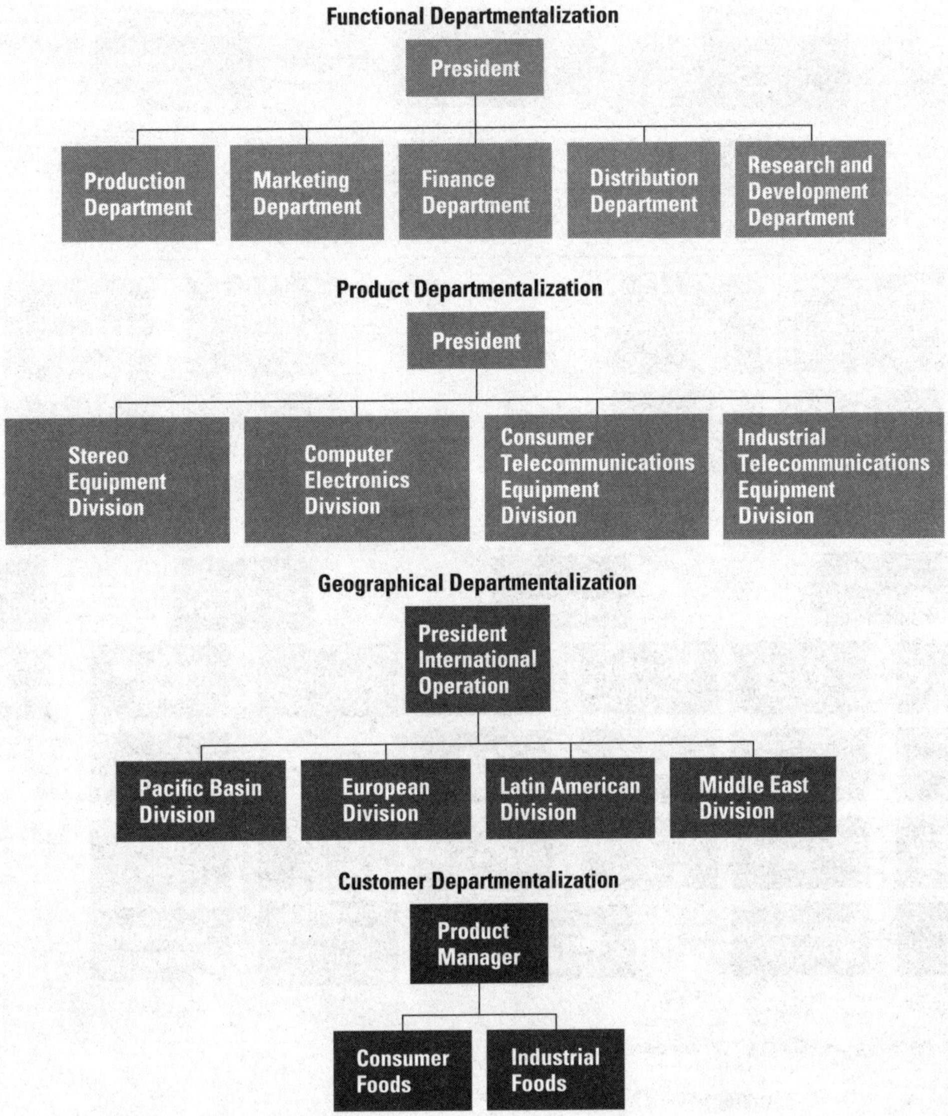

goods manufacturers have departments for specific product lines (beverages, frozen dinners, canned goods, and so on) as well as departments dealing with legal, purchasing, finance, human resources, and other business functions. For smaller companies, accounting can be set up online, almost as an automated department. Accounting software can handle electronic transfers so you never have to worry about a late bill. Many city governments also have departments for specific services (e.g., police, fire, waste disposal) as well as departments for legal, human resources, and other business functions. Figure 2.3 depicts the organizational chart for the city of Corpus Christi, Texas, showing these departments.

FIGURE 2.3 An Organizational Chart for the City of Corpus Christi

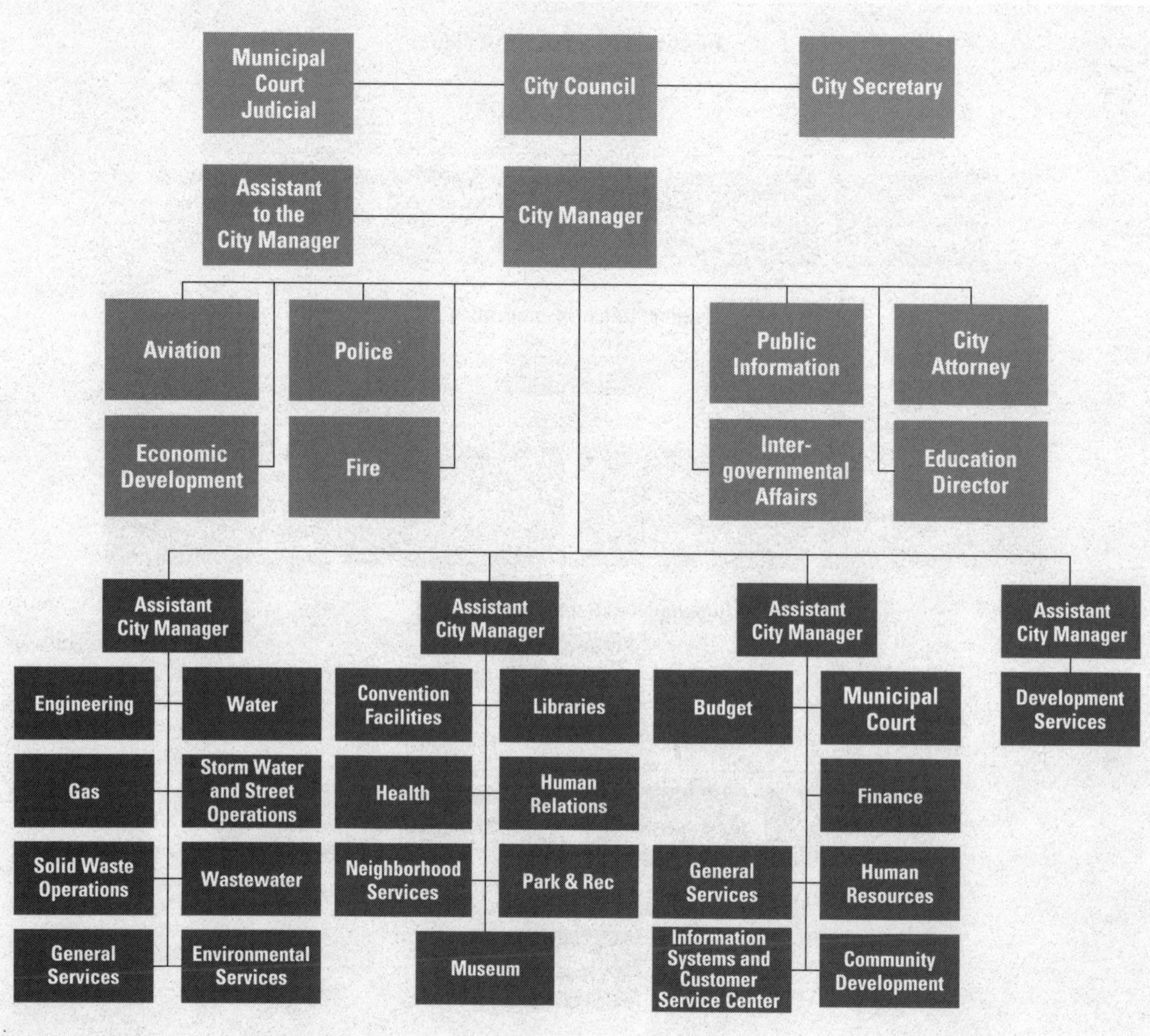

Source: "City of Corpus Christi Organizational Chart," City of Corpus Christi.

按职能划分部门
functional departmentalization
the grouping of jobs that perform similar functional activities, such as finance, manufacturing, marketing, and human resources

按职能划分部门

Functional Departmentalization. **Functional departmentalization** groups jobs that perform similar functional activities, such as finance, manufacturing, marketing, and human resources. Each of these functions is managed by an expert in the work done by the department—an engineer supervises the production department; a financial executive supervises the finance department. This approach is common in small organizations. Green Mountain Coffee is departmentalized into six functions: sales and marketing, operations, human resources, finance, information systems, and social responsibility. A weakness of functional departmentalization is that, because it tends to emphasize departmental units rather than the organization as a whole, decision making that involves more than one department may be slow, and it requires greater coordination. Thus, as businesses grow, they tend to adopt other approaches to organizing jobs.

按产品划分部门

Product Departmentalization. **Product departmentalization,** as you might guess, organizes jobs around the products of the firm. Unilever has global units, including personal care, foods, refreshment, and home care.[11] Each division develops and implements its own product plans, monitors the results, and takes corrective action as necessary. Functional activities—production, finance, marketing, and others—are located within each product division. Consequently, organizing by products duplicates functions and resources and emphasizes the product rather than achievement of the organization's overall objectives. However, it simplifies decision making and helps coordinate all activities related to a product or product group. PepsiCo Inc. is organized into four business units: (1) PepsiCo Americas Foods, which includes brands such as Frito-Lay North America, Quaker Foods North America, and all of its Latin American food and snack businesses; (2) PepsiCo Americas Beverages, which includes the Mountain Dew, Lipton, and Tropicana brands; (3) PepsiCo Europe, which includes regional brands like Wimm-Bill-Dann and Marbo as well as all beverage, food, and snack businesses in Europe and South Africa; and (4) PepsiCo Asia, Middle East and Africa, which includes all beverage, food, and snack businesses in these regions. PepsiCo has actually adopted a combination of two types of departmentalization. While it clearly separates foods from beverages in the Americas, the company chooses to divide its segments into geographic regions—a type of geographic departmentalization.[12]

按产品划分部门
product departmentalization
the organization of jobs in relation to the products of the firm

按地理区域划分部门

Geographical Departmentalization. **Geographical departmentalization** groups jobs according to geographic location, such as a state, region, country, or continent. Diageo, the premium beverage company known for brands such as Johnny Walker and Tanqueray, is organized into five geographic regions, allowing the company to get closer to its customers and respond more quickly and efficiently to regional competitors.[13] Multinational corporations often use a geographical approach because of vast differences between different regions. Coca-Cola, General Motors, and Caterpillar are organized by region. However, organizing by region requires a large administrative staff and control system to coordinate operations, and tasks are duplicated among the different regions.

按地理区域划分部门
geographical departmentalization
the grouping of jobs according to geographic location, such as state, region, country, or continent

按客户划分部门

Customer Departmentalization. **Customer departmentalization** arranges jobs around the needs of various types of customers. Proctor & Gamble, for example, recently restructured their business divisions according to types of customers: global baby, feminine and family care; global beauty; global health and grooming; and global fabric and home care. This allows the company to address the unique requirements of each group.[14] Airlines, such as British Airways and Delta, provide prices and services customized for either business/frequent travelers or infrequent/vacationing customers. Customer departmentalization, like geographical departmentalization, does not focus on the organization as a whole and therefore requires a large administrative staff to coordinate the operations of the various groups.

按客户划分部门
customer departmentalization
the arrangement of jobs around the needs of various types of customers

责任的分配
Assigning Responsibility

LO 2-3

After all workers and work groups have been assigned their tasks, they must be given the responsibility to carry them out. Management must determine to what extent it will delegate responsibility throughout the organization and how many employees will report to each manager.

授权
Delegation of Authority

授权
delegation of authority
giving employees not only tasks, but also the power to make commitments, use resources, and take whatever actions are necessary to carry out those tasks

Delegation of authority means not only giving tasks to employees but also empowering them to make commitments, use resources, and take whatever actions are necessary to carry out those tasks. Let's say a marketing manager at Nestlé has assigned an employee to design a new package that is less wasteful (more environmentally responsible) than the current package for one of the company's frozen dinner lines. To carry out the assignment, the employee needs access to information and the authority to make certain decisions on packaging materials, costs, and so on. Without the authority to carry out the assigned task, the employee would have to get the approval of others for every decision and every request for materials.

As a business grows, so do the number and complexity of decisions that must be made; no one manager can handle them all. Nordstrom delegates authority to its customer service personnel by telling them to use their best judgment when dealing with customers. This allows employees to offer the best tailored service to each individual customer and is one reason the retailer is known for its superior customer service.[15] Delegation of authority frees a manager to concentrate on larger issues, such as planning or dealing with problems and opportunities.

责任
responsibility
the obligation, placed on employees through delegation, to perform assigned tasks satisfactorily and be held accountable for the proper execution of work

问责制
accountability
the principle that employees who accept an assignment and the authority to carry it out are answerable to a superior for the outcome

Delegation also gives a **responsibility,** or obligation, to employees to carry out assigned tasks satisfactorily and holds them accountable for the proper execution of their assigned work. The principle of **accountability** means that employees who accept an assignment and the authority to carry it out are answerable to a superior for the outcome. Returning to the Nestlé example, if the packaging design prepared by the employee is unacceptable or late, the employee must accept the blame. If the new design is innovative, attractive, and cost-efficient, as well as environmentally responsible, or is completed ahead of schedule, the employee will accept the credit.

The process of delegating authority establishes a pattern of relationships and accountability between a superior and his or her subordinates. The president of a firm delegates responsibility for all marketing activities to the vice president of marketing. The vice president accepts this responsibility and has the authority to obtain all relevant information, make certain decisions, and delegate any or all activities to his or her subordinates. The vice president, in turn, delegates all advertising activities to the advertising manager, all sales activities to the sales manager, and so on. These managers then delegate specific tasks to their subordinates. However, the act of delegating authority to a subordinate does not relieve the superior of accountability for the delegated job. Even though the vice president of marketing delegates work to subordinates, he or she is still ultimately accountable to the president for all marketing activities.

集权程度
Degree of Centralization

The extent to which authority is delegated throughout an organization determines its degree of centralization.

集权制组织
centralized organization
a structure in which authority is concentrated at the top, and very little decision-making authority is delegated to lower levels

集权制组织
Centralized Organizations. In a **centralized organization,** authority is concentrated at the top, and very little decision-making authority is delegated to lower levels. Although decision-making authority in centralized organizations rests with top levels of management, a vast amount of responsibility for carrying out daily and routine procedures is delegated to even the lowest levels of the organization. Many government organizations, including the U.S. Army, the Postal Service, and the IRS, are centralized.

Businesses tend to be more centralized when the decisions to be made are risky and when low-level managers are not highly skilled in decision making. In the banking

Entrepreneurship in Action

Forming a Successful New Business: Group Collaboration

Nota Bene
Founders: Amy Bass and Evvy Diamond
Founded: 2007, in Aspinwall, Pennsylvania
Success: Through intense teamwork and collaboration, Nota Bene has become a successful stationery business with $500,000 in annual revenues.

The stationery shop Nota Bene was founded through the collaboration between the skills and interests of two friends, Amy Bass and Evvy Diamond. Diamond, who had had a lifelong attraction to stationery, started designing note cards when her children left for college. After an unsuccessful effort to sell her craft at a stationery show, she realized she needed a different outlet and a significant investment in order to properly sell her designs. Diamond sparked the interest of her friend Amy, who had business experience, and together they invested their money and started the business full-time in 2007. They formed a group with complementary skills in business and design and differentiated themselves from their competition by offering original designs, customization, and in-depth personal interaction with their customers. For instance, the entrepreneurs frequently meet with brides after-hours to go over their needs for wedding announcements. Five years after its creation, the company is generating $500,000 in annual revenues despite intense online competition.[16]

---

industry, for example, authority to make routine car loans is given to all loan managers, while the authority to make high-risk loans, such as for a large residential development, may be restricted to upper-level loan officers.

Overcentralization can cause serious problems for a company, in part because it may take longer for the organization as a whole to implement decisions and to respond to changes and problems on a regional scale. McDonald's, for example, was one of the last chains to introduce a chicken sandwich because of the amount of research, development, test marketing, and layers of approval the product had to go through.

分权制组织

Decentralized Organizations. A **decentralized organization** is one in which decision-making authority is delegated as far down the chain of command as possible. Decentralization is characteristic of organizations that operate in complex, unpredictable environments. Businesses that face intense competition often decentralize to improve responsiveness and enhance creativity. Lower-level managers who interact with the external environment often develop a good understanding of it and thus are able to react quickly to changes. Johnson & Johnson has a very decentralized, flat organizational structure.

分权制组织
decentralized organization
an organization in which decision-making authority is delegated as far down the chain of command as possible

Delegating authority to lower levels of managers may increase the organization's productivity. Decentralization requires that lower-level managers have strong decision-making skills. In recent years, the trend has been toward more decentralized organizations, and some of the largest and most successful companies, including GE, IBM, Google, and Nike, have decentralized decision-making authority. McDonald's, Taco Bell, and Pizza Hut have established themselves in the growing Indian market by decentralizing operations by varying products in specific markets to better meet customer demands. McDonald's, for example, has implemented spicy and vegetarian menu options in India to appeal to the native tastes. Becoming decentralized can be difficult for a fast-food restaurant that relies on standardized processes and core products. Burger King's core offering, the Whopper, will not likely be well accepted in India because beef is rarely eaten. Some suggest the chain should offer vegetarian pizza since it is popular in India. Diversity and decentralization are the keys to being better, not just bigger.[17] Nonprofit organizations benefit from decentralization as well.

管理幅度
Span of Management

How many subordinates should a manager manage? There is no simple answer. Experts generally agree, however, that top managers should not directly supervise more than four to eight people, while lower-level managers who supervise routine tasks are capable of managing a much larger number of subordinates. For example, the manager of the finance department may supervise 25 employees, whereas the vice president of finance may supervise only five managers. **Span of management** refers to the number of subordinates who report to a particular manager. A *wide span of management* exists when a manager directly supervises a very large number of employees. A *narrow span of management* exists when a manager directly supervises only a few subordinates (Figure 2.4). At Whole Foods, the best employees are recruited and placed in small teams. Employees are empowered to discount, give away, and sample products, as well as to assist in creating a respectful workplace where goals are achieved, individual employees succeed, and customers are core in business decisions. Whole Foods teams get to vote on new employee hires as well. This approach allows Whole Foods to offer unique and "local market" experiences in each of its stores. This level of customization is in contrast to more centralized national supermarket chains such as Kroger, Safeway, and Publix.[18]

管理幅度
span of management the number of subordinates who report to a particular manager

Should the span of management be wide or narrow? To answer this question, several factors need to be considered. A narrow span of management is appropriate when superiors and subordinates are not in close proximity, the manager has many responsibilities in addition to the supervision, the interaction between superiors and subordinates is frequent, and problems are common. However, when superiors and subordinates are located close to one another, the manager has few responsibilities other than supervision, the level of interaction between superiors and subordinates is low, few problems arise, subordinates are highly competent, and a set of specific operating procedures governs the activities of managers and their subordinates, a wide span of management will be more appropriate. Narrow spans of management are typical in centralized organizations, while wide spans of management are more common in decentralized firms.

组织层级
Organizational Layers

组织层级
organizational layers the levels of management in an organization

Complementing the concept of span of management is **organizational layers,** the levels of management in an organization. A company with many layers of managers is considered tall; in a tall organization, the span of management is narrow (see Figure 2.4). Because each manager supervises only a few subordinates, many

FIGURE 2.4
Span of Management: Wide Span and Narrow Span

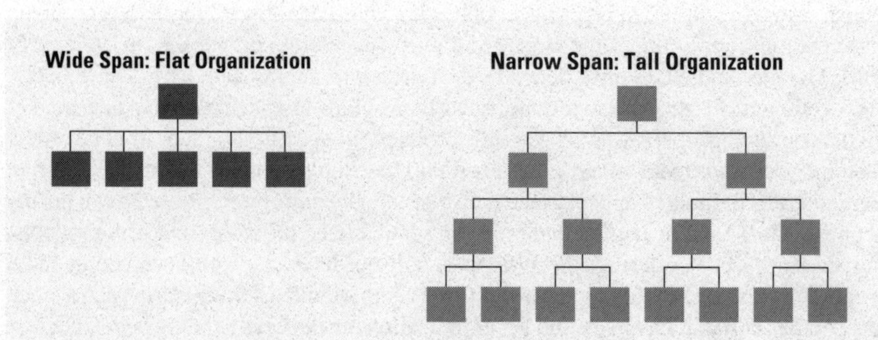

layers of management are necessary to carry out the operations of the business. McDonald's, for example, has a tall organization with many layers, including store managers, district managers, regional managers, and functional managers (finance, marketing, and so on), as well as a chief executive officer and many vice presidents. Because there are more managers in tall organizations than in flat organizations, administrative costs are usually higher. Communication is slower because information must pass through many layers.

Organizations with few layers are flat and have wide spans of management. When managers supervise a large number of employees, fewer management layers are needed to conduct the organization's activities. Managers in flat organizations typically perform more administrative duties than managers in tall organizations because there are fewer of them. They also spend more time supervising and working with subordinates.

Many of the companies that have decentralized also flattened their structures and widened their spans of management, often by eliminating layers of middle management. As mentioned earlier in this chapter, Johnson & Johnson has both a decentralized and flat organizational structure. Other corporations, including Avon, AT&T, and Ford Motor Company, embraced a more decentralized structure to reduce costs, speed up decision making, and boost overall productivity.

组织结构的形式
Forms of Organizational Structure

LO 2-4

Along with assigning tasks and the responsibility for carrying them out, managers must consider how to structure their authority relationships—that is, what structure the organization itself will have and how it will appear on the organizational chart. Common forms of organization include line structure, line-and-staff structure, multidivisional structure, and matrix structure.

直线式结构
Line Structure

The simplest organizational structure, **line structure,** has direct lines of authority that extend from the top manager to employees at the lowest level of the organization. For example, a convenience store employee at 7-Eleven may report to an assistant manager, who reports to the store manager, who reports to a regional manager, or, in an independent store, directly to the owner (Figure 2.5). This structure has a clear chain of command, which enables managers to make decisions quickly. A mid-level manager facing a decision must consult only one person, his or her immediate supervisor. However, this structure requires that managers possess a wide range of knowledge and skills. They are responsible for a variety of activities and must be knowledgeable about them all. Line structures are most common in small businesses.

直线式结构
line structure
the simplest organizational structure, in which direct lines of authority extend from the top manager to the lowest level of the organization

FIGURE 2.5 **Line Structure**

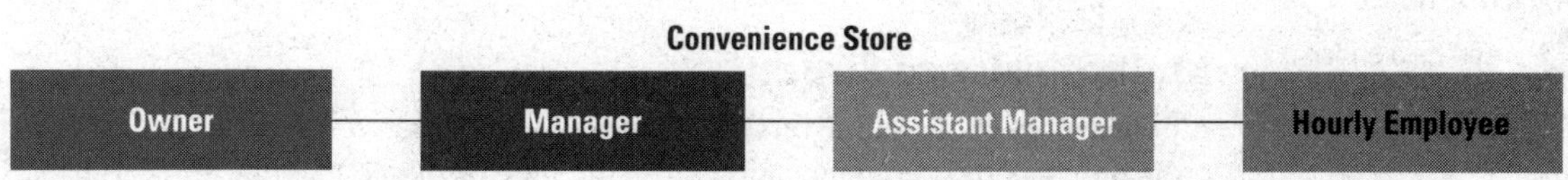

FIGURE 2.6
Line-and-Staff Structure

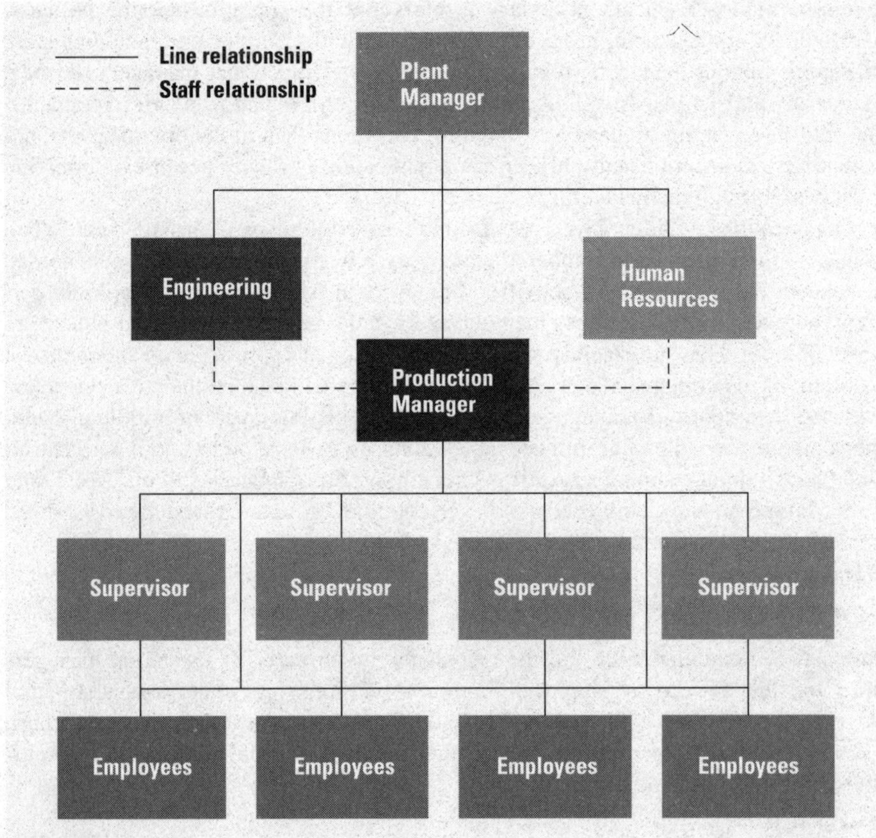

直线参谋式结构
line-and-staff structure
a structure having a traditional line relationship between superiors and subordinates and also specialized managers—called staff managers—who are available to assist line managers

直线参谋式结构
Line-and-Staff Structure

The **line-and-staff structure** has a traditional line relationship between superiors and subordinates, and specialized managers—called staff managers—are available to assist line managers (Figure 2.6). Line managers can focus on their area of expertise in the operation of the business, while staff managers provide advice and support to line departments on specialized matters such as finance, engineering, human resources, and the law. In the city of Corpus Christi (refer back for Figure 2.3), for example, assistant city managers are line managers who oversee groups of related departments. However, the city attorney, police chief, and fire chief are effectively staff managers who report directly to the city manager (the city equivalent of a business chief executive officer). Staff managers do not have direct authority over line managers or over the line manager's subordinates, but they do have direct authority over subordinates in their own departments. However, line-and-staff organizations may experience problems with overstaffing and ambiguous lines of communication. Additionally, employees may become frustrated because they lack the authority to carry out certain decisions.

connect

Need help understanding Line vs. Staff Employees? Visit your Connect ebook video tab for a brief animated explanation.

多事业部制结构
Multidivisional Structure

As companies grow and diversify, traditional line structures become difficult to coordinate, making communication difficult and decision making slow. When the weaknesses of the structure—the "turf wars," miscommunication, and working at cross-purposes—exceed the benefits, growing firms tend to restructure, often into the divisionalized form. A **multidivisional structure** organizes departments into larger groups called divisions. Just as departments might be formed on the basis of geography, customer, product, or a combination of these, so too divisions can be formed based on any of these methods of organizing. Within each of these divisions, departments may be organized by product, geographic region, function, or some combination of all three. Indra Nooyi, CEO of PepsiCo, rearranged the company's organizational structure. Prior to her tenure, PepsiCo was organized geographically. She created new units—PepsiCo Americas Foods (PAF), PepsiCo Americas Beverages (PAB), PepsiCo Europe, and PepsiCo Asia, Middle East & Africa—that span international boundaries and make it easier for employees in different geographic regions to share business practices.[19]

多事业部制结构
multidivisional structure
a structure that organizes departments into larger groups called divisions

Multidivisional structures permit delegation of decision-making authority, allowing divisional and department managers to specialize. They allow those closest to the action to make the decisions that will affect them. Delegation of authority and divisionalized work also mean that better decisions are made faster, and they tend to be more innovative. Most importantly, by focusing each division on a common region, product, or customer, each is more likely to provide products that meet the needs of its particular customers. However, the divisional structure inevitably creates work duplication, which makes it more difficult to realize the economies of scale that result from grouping functions together.

矩阵式结构
Matrix Structure

Another structure that attempts to address issues that arise with growth, diversification, productivity, and competitiveness, is the matrix. A **matrix structure,** also called a project management structure, sets up teams from different departments, thereby creating two or more intersecting lines of authority (Figure 2.7). One of the first

矩阵式结构
matrix structure
a structure that sets up teams from different departments, thereby creating two or more intersecting lines of authority; also called a project-management structure

FIGURE 2.7
Matrix Structure

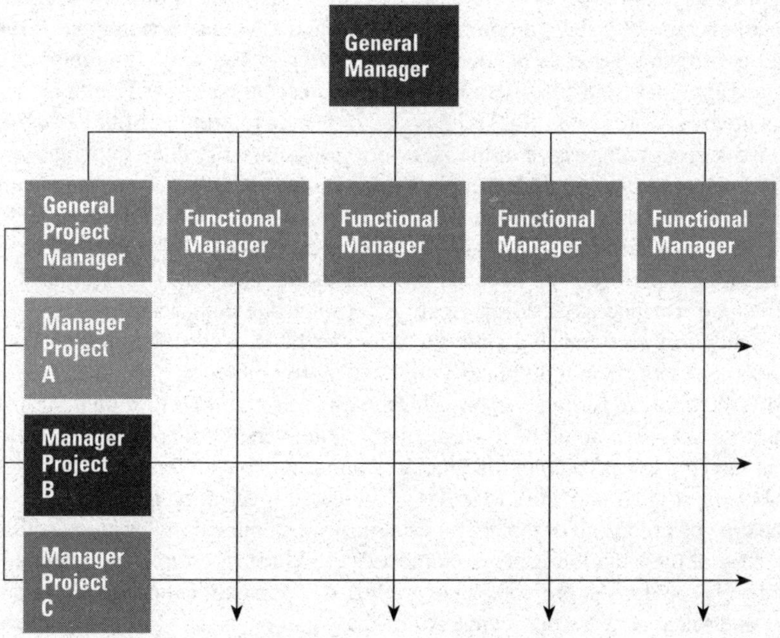

organizations to design and implement a matrix structure was the National Aeronautics and Space Administration (NASA) for the space program because it needed to coordinate different projects at the same time. The matrix structure superimposes project-based departments on the more traditional, function-based departments. Project teams bring together specialists from a variety of areas to work together on a single project, such as developing a new fighter jet. In this arrangement, employees are responsible to two managers—functional managers and project managers. Matrix structures are usually temporary: Team members typically go back to their functional or line department after a project is finished. However, more firms are becoming permanent matrix structures, creating and dissolving project teams as needed to meet customer needs. The aerospace industry was one of the first to apply the matrix structure, but today it is used by universities and schools, accounting firms, banks, and organizations in other industries.

Matrix structures provide flexibility, enhanced cooperation, and creativity, and they enable the company to respond quickly to changes in the environment by giving special attention to specific projects or problems. However, they are generally expensive and quite complex, and employees may be confused as to whose authority has priority—the project manager's or the immediate supervisor's.

LO 2-5

小组与团队在组织中的角色
The Role of Groups and Teams in Organizations

Regardless of how they are organized, most of the essential work of business occurs in individual work groups and teams, so we'll take a closer look at them now. Although some experts do not make a distinction between groups and teams, in recent years there has been a gradual shift toward an emphasis on teams and managing them to enhance individual and organizational success. Some experts now believe that highest productivity results only when groups become teams.[20]

小组
group
two or more individuals who communicate with one another, share a common identity, and have a common goal

团队
team
a small group whose members have complementary skills; have a common purpose, goals, and approach; and hold themselves mutually accountable

Traditionally, a **group** has been defined as two or more individuals who communicate with one another, share a common identity, and have a common goal. A **team** is a small group whose members have complementary skills; have a common purpose, goals, and approach; and hold themselves mutually accountable.[21] All teams are groups, but not all groups are teams. Table 2.2 points out some important differences between them. Work groups emphasize individual work products, individual accountability, and even individual leadership. Salespeople working independently for the same company could be a work group. In contrast, work teams share leadership roles, have both individual and mutual accountability, and create collective work products. In other words, a work group's performance depends on what its members do as individuals, while a team's performance is based on creating a knowledge center and a competency to work together to accomplish a goal. On the other hand, it is also important for team members to retain their individuality and avoid becoming just "another face in the crowd." According to former corporate lawyer and negotiations consultant Susan Cain, the purpose of teams should be toward collaboration versus collectivism. Although the team is working toward a common goal, it is important that all team members actively contribute their ideas and work together to achieve this common goal.[22]

The type of groups an organization establishes depends on the tasks it needs to accomplish and the situation it faces. Some specific kinds of groups and teams include committees, task forces, project teams, product-development teams, quality-assurance teams, and self-directed work teams. All of these can be *virtual teams*—employees in

TABLE 2.2
Differences between Groups and Teams

Working Group	Team
Has strong, clearly focused leader	Has shared leadership roles
Has individual accountability	Has individual and group accountability
Has the same purpose as the broader organizational mission	Has a specific purpose that the team itself delivers
Creates individual work products	Creates collective work products
Runs efficient meetings	Encourages open-ended discussion and active problem-solving meetings
Measures its effectiveness indirectly by its effects on others (e.g., financial performance of the business)	Measures performance directly by assessing collective work products
Discusses, decides, and delegates	Discusses, decides, and does real work together

Source: Robert Gatewood, Robert Taylor, and O. C. Ferrell, Management: Comprehension Analysis and Application, *1995, p. 427.*

different locations who rely on e-mail, audio conferencing, fax, Internet, videoconferencing, or other technological tools to accomplish their goals. Virtual teams are becoming a part of everyday business, with the number of employees working remotely from their employer increasing more than 80 percent in the last several years.[23] Virtual teams have also opened up opportunities for different companies. Not only does Cisco Systems Inc. work in virtual teams, but the company makes networking technology to support video conferencing. At Cisco Europe, 10,000 employees across 21 countries developed a set of team operating principles to aid team collaboration.[24]

委员会
Committees

A **committee** is usually a permanent, formal group that does some specific task. For example, many firms have a compensation or finance committee to examine the effectiveness of these areas of operation as well as the need for possible changes. Ethics committees are formed to develop and revise codes of ethics, suggest methods for implementing ethical standards, and review specific issues and concerns.

委员会
committee
a permanent, formal group that performs a specific task

特别工作组
Task Forces

A **task force** is a temporary group of employees responsible for bringing about a particular change. They typically come from across all departments and levels of an organization. Task force membership is usually based on expertise rather than organizational position. Occasionally, a task force may be formed from individuals outside a company. Coca-Cola has often used task forces to address problems and provide recommendations for improving company practices or products. While some task forces might last a few months, others last for years. When Coca-Cola faced lawsuits alleging discrimination practices in hiring and promotion, it developed a five-year task force to examine pay and promotion practices among minority employees. Its experiences helped Coca-Cola realize the advantages of having a cross-functional task force made up of employees from different departments, and it continued to use task forces to

特别工作组
task force
a temporary group of employees responsible for bringing about a particular change

At Google, small teams work on research and engineering projects that often last 6–12 months.

tackle major company issues. Other companies that have also recognized the benefits of task forces include IBM, Prudential, and General Electric.[25]

团队

Teams

Teams are becoming far more common in the U.S. workplace as businesses strive to enhance productivity and global competitiveness. In general, teams have the benefit of being able to pool members' knowledge and skills and make greater use of them than can individuals working alone. Team building is becoming increasingly popular in organizations, with around half of executives indicating their companies had team-building training. Teams require harmony, cooperation, synchronized effort, and flexibility to maximize their contribution.[26] Teams can also create more solutions to problems than can individuals. Furthermore, team participation enhances employee acceptance of, understanding of, and commitment to team goals. Teams motivate workers by providing internal rewards in the form of an enhanced sense of accomplishment for employees as they achieve more, and external rewards in the form of praise and certain perks. Consequently, they can help get workers more involved. They can help companies be more innovative, and they can boost productivity and cut costs.

According to psychologist Ivan Steiner, team productivity peaks at about five team members. People become less motivated and group coordination becomes more difficult after this size. Jeff Bezos, Amazon.com CEO, says that he has a "two-pizza rule": If a team cannot be fed by two pizzas, it is too large. Keep teams small enough where everyone gets a piece of the action.[27]

项目团队
project teams
groups similar to task forces that normally run their operation and have total control of a specific work project

产品开发团队
product-development teams
a specific type of project team formed to devise, design, and implement a new product

质量保证团队
quality-assurance teams (or quality circles)
small groups of workers brought together from throughout the organization to solve specific quality, productivity, or service problems

项目团队

Project Teams. **Project teams** are similar to task forces, but normally they run their operation and have total control of a specific work project. Like task forces, their membership is likely to cut across the firm's hierarchy and be composed of people from different functional areas. They are almost always temporary, although a large project, such as designing and building a new airplane at Boeing Corporation, may last for years.

Product-development teams are a special type of project team formed to devise, design, and implement a new product. Sometimes product-development teams exist within a functional area—research and development—but now they more frequently include people from numerous functional areas and may even include customers to help ensure that the end product meets the customers' needs. Intel informs their product development process through indirect input from customers. They have a social scientist on staff who leads a research team on how customers actually use products. This is done mainly by observation and asking questions. Once enough information is gathered, it is relayed to the product-development team and incorporated into their designs.[28]

质量保证团队

Quality-Assurance Teams. **Quality-assurance teams,** sometimes called **quality circles,** are fairly small groups of workers brought together from throughout the organization to solve specific quality, productivity, or service problems. Although the *quality circle* term is not as popular as it once was, the concern about quality is stronger than ever. Companies such as IBM and Xerox as well as companies in the

Going Green

Numi Organic Tea Utilizes Teamwork to Increase Sustainability Initiatives

Numi Organic Tea was organized as a Benefit (B) corporation in 1999 in Oakland, California. This benefit status is a certification that implies the company adheres to strict environmental and socially responsible standards. Numi, a dried lime that can be brewed as tea, is a staple in Iraq, the native home of the founders: brother-and-sister team Ahmed and Reem Rahim. The company incorporates the quadruple bottom line (people, planet, product, and profit) into their business model with organic tea that is completely natural and ethically and environmentally sourced. In reaching their shared goals, the founders quickly learned that effective communication is a vital component. Having different communication styles, Ahmed taught Reem to be more outspoken with her ideas and criticisms, while Reem taught Ahmed the value of listening to others and considering their opinions.

They translated these lessons externally to build partnerships with various Fair Trade organizations to extend their reach. As a result, Numi became one of the world's leaders in importing Fair Trade–certified organic tea and achieved annual sales of more than $20 million with a presence in almost 40 countries. Face-to-face communication is heavily emphasized by the company. The founders frequently travel to the farms where the tea leaves are sourced to make sure farmers are receiving competitive compensation and Fair Trade standards are met.

Their values are also apparent in their packaging. Numi became the first company to receive verification of its packaging and tea bags by the Non-GMO Project with its all-natural, completely recyclable, and biodegradable hemp-based tea bags that are printed with soy-based inks. Many companies, especially in the United States, make packaging and tea bags from genetically modified materials such as genetically modified corn and petroleum-based nylon.[29]

automobile industry have used quality circles to shift the organization to a more participative culture. The use of teams to address quality issues will no doubt continue to increase throughout the business world.

自主工作团队

Self-directed Work Teams. A **self-directed work team (SDWT)** is a group of employees responsible for an entire work process or segment that delivers a product to an internal or external customer.[30] SDWTs permit the flexibility to change rapidly to meet the competition or respond to customer needs. The defining characteristic of an SDWT is the extent to which it is empowered or given authority to make and implement work decisions. Thus, SDWTs are designed to give employees a feeling of "ownership" of a whole job. Employees at 3M as well as an increasing number of companies encourage employees to be active to perform a function or operational task. With shared team responsibility for work outcomes, team members often have broader job assignments and cross-train to master other jobs, thus permitting greater team flexibility.

自主工作团队
self-directed work team (SDWT)
a group of employees responsible for an entire work process or segment that delivers a product to an internal or external customer

组织中的沟通
Communicating in Organizations

LO 2-6

Communication within an organization can flow in a variety of directions and from a number of sources, each using both oral and written forms of communication. The success of communication systems within the organization has a tremendous effect on the overall success of the firm. Communication mistakes can lower productivity and morale.

Alternatives to face-to-face communications—such as meetings—are growing, thanks to technology such as voice-mail, e-mail, social media, and online newsletters. Many companies use internal networks called intranets

DID YOU KNOW? A survey of managers and executives found that they feel 28 percent of meetings are a waste of time and that information could be communicated more effectively using other methods.[31]

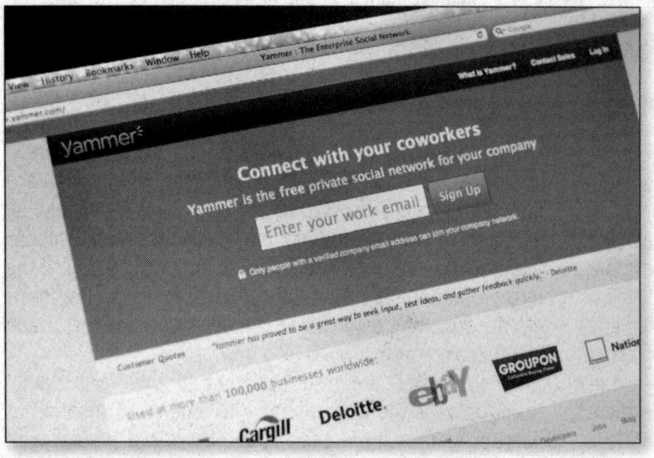

Yammer is a social network that companies can use to connect employees with one another.

to share information with employees. Intranets increase communication across different departments and levels of management and help with the flow of everyday business activities. Another innovative approach is cloud computing. Rather than using physical products, companies using cloud computing technology can access computing resources and information over a network. Cloud computing allows companies to have more control over computing resources and can be less expensive than hardware or software. Salesforce.com uses cloud computing in its customer relationship management solutions.[32] Companies can even integrate aspects of social media into their intranets, allowing employees to post comments and pictures, participate in polls, and create group calendars. However, increased access to the Internet at work has also created many problems, including employee abuse of company email and Internet access.[33]

正式沟通

Formal Communication

Formal channels of communication are intentionally defined and designed by the organization. They represent the flow of communication within the formal organizational structure, as shown on organizational charts. Traditionally, formal communication patterns were classified as vertical and horizontal, but with the increased use of teams and matrix structures, formal communication may occur in a number of patterns (Figure 2.8).

Upward communication flows from lower to higher levels of the organization and includes information such as progress reports, suggestions for improvement, inquiries, and grievances. *Downward communication* refers to the traditional flow of

FIGURE 2.8
The Flow of Communication in an Organizational Hierarchy

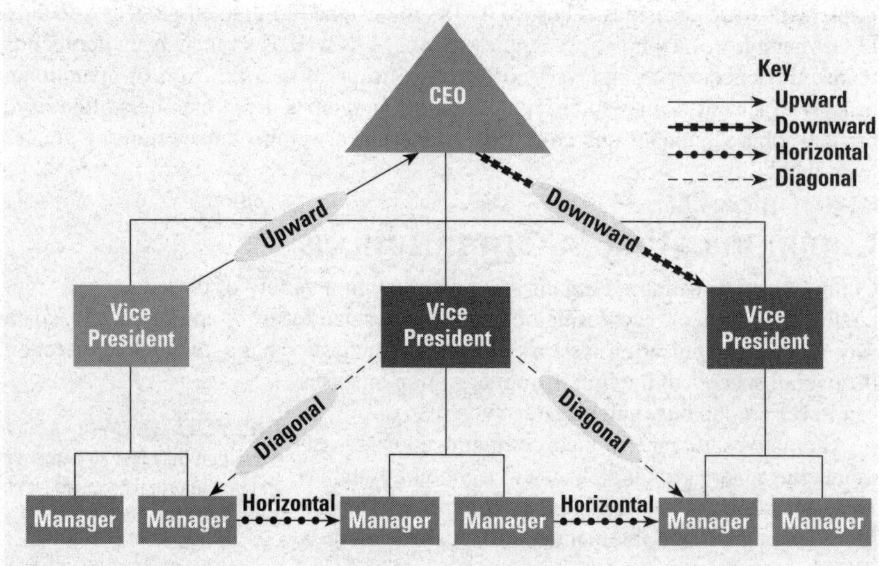

information from upper organizational levels to lower levels. This type of communication typically involves directions, the assignment of tasks and responsibilities, performance feedback, and certain details about the organization's strategies and goals. Speeches, policy and procedures manuals, employee handbooks, company leaflets, telecommunications, and job descriptions are examples of downward communication.

Horizontal communication involves the exchange of information among colleagues and peers on the same organizational level, such as across or within departments. Horizontal information informs, supports, and coordinates activities both within the department and with other departments. At times, the business will formally require horizontal communication among particular organizational members, as is the case with task forces or project teams.

With more and more companies downsizing and increasing the use of self-managed work teams, many workers are being required to communicate with others in different departments and on different levels to solve problems and coordinate work. When these individuals from different units and organizational levels communicate, it is *diagonal communication.*

非正式沟通渠道
Informal Communication Channels

Along with the formal channels of communication shown on an organizational chart, all firms communicate informally as well. Communication between friends, for instance, cuts across department, division, and even management–subordinate boundaries. Such friendships and other nonwork social relationships comprise the *informal organization* of a firm, and their impact can be great.

The most significant informal communication occurs through the **grapevine,** an informal channel of communication, separate from management's formal, official communication channels. Grapevines exist in all organizations. Information passed along the grapevine may relate to the job or organization, or it may be gossip and rumors unrelated to either. The accuracy of grapevine information has been of great concern to managers.

小道消息
grapevine
an informal channel of communication, separate from management's formal, official communication channels

Additionally, managers can turn the grapevine to their advantage. Using it as a "sounding device" for possible new policies is one example. Managers can obtain valuable information from the grapevine that could improve decision making. Some organizations use the grapevine to their advantage by floating ideas, soliciting feedback, and reacting accordingly. People love to gossip, and managers need to be aware that grapevines exist in every organization. Managers who understand how the grapevine works also can use it to their advantage by feeding it facts to squelch rumors and incorrect information.

对沟通的监控
Monitoring Communications

Technological advances and the increased use of electronic communication in the workplace have made monitoring its use necessary for most companies. Failing to monitor employees' use of e-mail, social media, and the Internet can be costly. Many companies require that employees sign and follow a policy on appropriate Internet use. These agreements often require that employees will use corporate computers only for work-related activities. Additionally, several companies use software programs to monitor employee computer usage.[34] Instituting practices that show respect for employee privacy but do not abdicate employer responsibility are increasingly necessary in today's workplace. Several websites provide model policies and detailed guidelines for conducting electronic monitoring, including the Model Electronic Privacy Act on the American Civil Liberties Union site.

提高沟通效率
Improving Communication Effectiveness

Without effective communication, the activities and overall productivity of projects, groups, teams, and individuals will be diminished. Communication is an important area for a firm to address at all levels of management. Apple supplier Foxconn is one example of how essential communication is to a firm. Despite criticisms of unfair labor conditions, the Fair Labor Association determined that Foxconn had formal procedures in place at its factories to prevent many major accidents. However, it concluded that the firm had a communication problem. These procedures were not being communicated to the factory workers, contributing to unsafe practices and two tragic explosions.[35]

One of the major issues of effective communication is in obtaining feedback. If feedback is not provided, then communication will be ineffective and can drag down overall performance. Managers should always encourage feedback, including concerns and challenges about issues. Listening is a skill that involves hearing, and most employees listen much more than they actively communicate to others. Therefore, managers should encourage employees to provide feedback—even if it is negative. This will allow the organization to identify strengths and weaknesses and make adjustments when needed. At the same time, strong feedback mechanisms help to empower employees as they feel that their voices are being heard.

Interruptions can be a serious threat to effective communication. Various activities can interrupt the message. For example, interjecting a remark can create discontinuance in the communication process or disrupt the uniformity of the message. Even small interruptions can be a problem if the messenger cannot adequately understand or interpret the communicator's message. One suggestion is to give the communicator space or time to make another statement rather than quickly responding or making your own comment.

Strong and effective communication channels are a requirement for companies to distribute information to different levels of the company. Businesses have several channels for communication, including face-to-face, e-mail, phone, and written communication (for example, memos). Each channel has advantages and disadvantages, and some are more appropriate to use than others. For instance, a small task requiring little instruction might be communicated through a short memo or e-mail. An in-depth task would most likely require a phone conversation or face-to-face contact. E-mail has become especially helpful for businesses, and both employees and managers are increasingly using e-mail rather than memos or phone conversations. However, it is important that employees use e-mail correctly. It is quite easy to send the wrong e-mail to the wrong person, and messages sent over e-mail can be misinterpreted. Inappropriate e-mails can be forwarded without a second thought, and employees have gotten in trouble for sending personal e-mails in the workplace. It is therefore important for companies to communicate their e-mail policies throughout the organization. Communicators using e-mail, whether managers or employees, must exert caution before pushing that "Send" button.

Communication is necessary in helping every organizational member understand what is expected of him or her. Many business problems can be avoided if clear communication exists within the company. Even the best business strategies are of little use if those who will oversee them cannot understand what is intended. Communication might not seem to be as big of a concern to management as finances, human resources, and marketing, but in reality it can make the difference between successful implementation of business activities or failure.

So You Want a Job in Managing Organizational Culture, Teamwork, and Communication

Jobs dealing with organizational culture and structure are usually at the top of the organization. If you want to be a CEO or high-level manager, you will help shape these areas of business. On the other hand, if you are an entrepreneur or small-business person, you will need to make decisions about assigning tasks, departmentalization, and assigning responsibility. Even managers in small organizations have to make decisions about decentralization, span of management, and forms of organizational structure. While these decisions may be part of your job, there are usually no job titles dealing with these specific areas. Specific jobs that attempt to improve organizational culture could include ethics and compliance positions as well as those who are in charge of communicating memos, manuals, and policies that help establish the culture. These positions will be in communications, human resources, and positions that assist top organizational managers.

Teams are becoming more common in the workplace, and it is possible to become a member of a product development group or quality assurance team. There are also human resource positions that encourage teamwork through training activities. The area of corporate communications provides lots of opportunities for specific jobs that facilitate communication systems. Thanks to technology, there are job positions to help disseminate information through online newsletters, intranets, or internal computer networks to share information to increase collaboration. In addition to the many advances using electronic communications, there are technology concerns that create new job opportunities. Monitoring workplace communications such as the use of e-mail and the Internet has created new industries. There have to be internal controls in the organization to make sure that the organization does not engage in any copyright infringement. If this is an area of interest, there are specific jobs that provide an opportunity to use your technological skills to assist in maintaining appropriate standards in communicating and using technology.

If you go to work for a large company with many divisions, you can expect a number of positions dealing with the tasks discussed here. If you go to work for a small company, you will probably engage in most of these tasks as a part of your position. Organizational flexibility requires individual flexibility, and those employees willing to take on new domains and challenges will be the employees who survive and prosper in the future.

Review Your Understanding

Define organizational structure, and relate how organizational structures develop.

Structure is the arrangement or relationship of positions within an organization; it develops when managers assign work activities to work groups and specific individuals and coordinate the diverse activities required to attain organizational objectives. Organizational structure evolves to accommodate growth, which requires people with specialized skills.

Describe how specialization and departmentalization help an organization achieve its goals.

Structuring an organization requires that management assign work tasks to specific individuals and groups. Under specialization, managers break labor into small, specialized tasks and assign employees to do a single task, fostering efficiency. Departmentalization is the grouping of jobs into working units (departments, units, groups, or divisions). Businesses may departmentalize by function, product, geographic region, or customer, or they may combine two or more of these.

Distinguish between groups and teams, and identify the types of groups that exist in organizations.

A group is two or more persons who communicate, share a common identity, and have a common goal. A team is a small group whose members have complementary skills, a common purpose, goals, and approach and who hold themselves mutually accountable. The major distinction is that individual performance is most important in groups, while collective work group performance counts most in teams. Special kinds of groups include task forces, committees, project teams, product-development teams, quality-assurance teams, and self-directed work teams.

Determine how organizations assign responsibility for tasks and delegate authority.

Delegation of authority means assigning tasks to employees and giving them the power to make commitments, use resources, and take whatever actions are necessary to accomplish the tasks. It lays responsibility on employees to carry out assigned tasks satisfactorily and holds them accountable to a superior for the proper execution of their assigned work. The extent to which authority is delegated throughout an organization determines its degree of centralization. Span of management refers to the number of subordinates who report to a particular manager. A wide span of management occurs in flat organizations; a narrow one exists in tall organizations.

Compare and contrast some common forms of organizational structure.

Line structures have direct lines of authority that extend from the top manager to employees at the lowest level of the organization. The line-and-staff structure has a traditional line relationship between superiors and subordinates, and specialized staff managers are available to assist line managers. A multidivisional structure gathers departments into larger groups called divisions. A matrix, or project-management, structure sets up teams from different departments, thereby creating two or more intersecting lines of authority.

Describe how communication occurs in organizations.

Communication occurs both formally and informally in organizations. Formal communication may be downward, upward, horizontal, and even diagonal. Informal communication takes place through friendships and the grapevine.

Analyze a business's use of teams.

"Solve the Dilemma" on page 228 introduces a firm attempting to restructure to a team environment. Based on the material presented in this chapter, you should be able to evaluate the firm's efforts and make recommendations for resolving the problems that have developed.

Revisit the World of Business

1. How does CarMax encourage employees to put customer needs first?
2. How has CarMax developed a decentralized culture?
3. Describe some ways that CarMax empowers its employees.

Learn the Terms

accountability
centralized organization
committee
customer departmentalization
decentralized organization
delegation of authority
departmentalization
functional departmentalization
geographical departmentalization
grapevine
group
line-and-staff structure
line structure
matrix structure
multidivisional structure
organizational chart
organizational culture
organizational layers
product departmentalization
product-development teams
project teams
quality-assurance teams (or quality circles)
responsibility
self-directed work team (SDWT)
span of management
specialization
structure
task force
team

Check Your Progress

1. Identify four types of departmentalization and give an example of each type.
2. Explain the difference between groups and teams.
3. What are self-managed work teams and what tasks might they perform that traditionally are performed by managers?
4. Explain how delegating authority, responsibility, and accountability are related.
5. Distinguish between centralization and decentralization. Under what circumstances is each appropriate?
6. Define span of management. Why do some organizations have narrow spans and others wide spans?
7. Discuss the different forms of organizational structure. What are the primary advantages and disadvantages of each form?
8. Discuss the role of the grapevine within organizations. How can managers use it to further the goals of the firm?
9. How have technological advances made electronic oversight a necessity in many companies?
10. Discuss how an organization's culture might influence its ability to achieve its objectives. Do you think that managers can "manage" the organization's culture?

Get Involved

1. Explain, using a specific example (perhaps your own future business), how an organizational structure might evolve. How would you handle the issues of specialization, delegation of authority, and centralization? Which structure would you use? Explain your answers.
2. Interview the department chairperson in charge of one of the academic departments in your college or university. Using Table 2.2 as a guideline, explore whether the professors function more like a group or a team. Contrast what you find here with what you see on your school's basketball, football, or baseball team.

Build Your Skills

Teamwork

Background

Think about all the different kinds of groups and teams you have been a member of or been involved with. Here's a checklist to help you remember them—with "Other" spaces to fill in ones not listed. Check all that apply.

School Groups/Teams	Community Groups/Teams	Employment Groups/Teams
☐ Sports teams	☐ Fund-raising groups	☐ Problem-solving teams
☐ Cheerleading squads	☐ Religious groups	☐ Work committees
☐ Musical groups	☐ Sports teams	☐ Project teams
☐ Hobby clubs	☐ Political groups	☐ Labor union groups
☐ Foreign language clubs	☐ Boy/Girl Scout troops	☐ Work crews
☐ Study groups	☐ Volunteer organizations	☐ Other _____
☐ Other _____	☐ Other _____	

Task

1. Of those you checked, circle those that you would categorize as a "really great team."
2. Examine the following table[36] and circle those characteristics from columns two and three that were represented in your "really great" team experiences.

Indicator	Good Team Experience	Not-So-Good Team Experience
Members arrive on time?	Members are prompt because they know others will be.	Members drift in sporadically, and some leave early.
Members prepared?	Members are prepared and know what to expect.	Members are unclear what the agenda is.
Meeting organized?	Members follow a planned agenda.	The agenda is tossed aside, and free-wheeling discussion ensues.
Members contribute equally?	Members give each other a chance to speak; quiet members are encouraged.	Some members always dominate the discussion; some are reluctant to speak their minds.
Discussions help members make decisions?	Members learn from others' points of view, new facts are discussed, creative ideas evolve, and alternatives emerge.	Members reinforce their belief in their own points of view, or their decisions were made long before the meeting.

Indicator	Good Team Experience	Not-So-Good Team Experience
Any disagreement?	Members follow a conflict-resolution process established as part of the team's policies.	Conflict turns to argument, angry words, emotion, blaming.
More cooperation or more conflict?	Cooperation is clearly an important ingredient.	Conflict flares openly, as well as simmering below the surface.
Commitment to decisions?	Members reach consensus before leaving.	Compromise is the best outcome possible; some members don't care about the result.
Member feelings after team decision?	Members are satisfied and are valued for their ideas.	Members are glad it's over, not sure of results or outcome.
Members support decision afterward?	Members are committed to implementation.	Some members second-guess or undermine the team's decision.

3. What can you take with you from your positive team experiences and apply to a work-related group or team situation in which you might be involved? ______________________

Solve the Dilemma LO 2-7

Quest Star in Transition

Quest Star (QS), which manufactures quality stereo loudspeakers, wants to improve its ability to compete against Japanese firms. Accordingly, the company has launched a comprehensive quality-improvement program for its Iowa plant. The QS Intracommunication Leadership Initiative (ILI) has flattened the layers of management. The program uses teams and peer pressure to accomplish the plant's goals instead of multiple management layers with their limited opportunities for communication. Under the initiative, employees make all decisions within the boundaries of their responsibilities, and they elect team representatives to coordinate with other teams. Teams are also assigned tasks ranging from establishing policies to evaluating on-the-job safety.

However, employees who are not self-motivated team players are having difficulty getting used to their peers' authority within this system. Upper-level managers face stress and frustration because they must train workers to supervise themselves.

Discussion Questions

1. What techniques or skills should an employee have to assume a leadership role within a work group?
2. If each work group has a team representative, what problems will be faced in supervising these representatives?
3. Evaluate the pros and cons of the system developed by QS.

Build Your Business Plan

Organization, Teamwork, and Communication

Developing a business plan as a team is a deliberate move of your instructor to encourage you to familiarize yourself with the concept of teamwork. You need to realize that you are going to spend a large part of your professional life working with others. At this point in time, you are working on the business plan for a grade, but after graduation, you will be "teaming" with coworkers and the success of your endeavor may determine whether you get a raise or a bonus. It is important that you be comfortable as soon as possible with working with others and holding them accountable for their contributions.

Some people are natural "leaders," and leaders often feel that if team members are not doing their work, they take it upon themselves to "do it all." This is not leadership, but rather micro-managing.

Leadership means holding members accountable for their responsibilities. Your instructor may provide ideas on how this could be implemented, possibly by utilizing peer reviews. Remember, you are not doing a team member a favor by doing their work for them.

If you are a "follower" (someone who takes directions well) rather than a leader, try to get into a team where others are hard workers and you will rise to their level. There is nothing wrong with being a follower; not everyone can be a leader!

See for Yourself Videocase

Zappos Creates Organizational Structure and Culture with Teams

Zappos began in 1999 as an online shoe retailer but has expanded into many product categories since then. The company has always taken pride in its focus on employees and customers and, as a result, has adopted a team structure to reinforce the kind of organizational culture for which it aims. Jeanne Markel, the director of the Downtown Team, states that the managerial goal "is to drive the culture within Zappos." As Zappos began incorporating more product categories, the teams grew both in size and number. This helped to reduce the complexity of company growth and establish a basis for success. Many companies utilize functional departmentalization as a structure to organize their activities. Zappos' many teams serve this same purpose but are described as teams rather than departments. This means that there is a team for each function under each product category, and if the product category is large enough, there will be teams for product subcategories.

While the company is run by teams in every department, one of the most important teams is the merchandising team, because team members are responsible for purchasing all inventory on the Zappos website. This team has approximately 200 people and is led by the Vice President of Merchandising. Under the VP is a Senior Director of Clothing and a General Manager of Footwear, who lead the directors responsible for each purchasing category, including clothing, fashion, and couture and accessories, as well as private-label, performance, and casual lifestyle categories. A team that encompasses such a large and integral responsibility to Zappos' business model will likely change structure to accommodate growth. For example, over the course of seven years, Jeanne Markel saw her team grow from 4 people to 27.

Each purchasing category is composed of its own team as well. The casual lifestyle category, for instance, is led by the Director of Merchandising, who manages four directors responsible for separate subcategories, including kids, comfort, size and width, and home and luggage. There is also a Lead Buyer for each subcategory. From here, the subcategories are divided into further categories. The kids category has a kids footwear merchandising team. The structure of this team begins with entry level Merchandising Assistants, who work closely with the next level of Assistant Buyers to learn the industry and the trade. Assistant Buyers are responsible for mentoring Merchandising Assistants as well as handling up to 15 brands and making decisions on purchases. The next level consists of Buyers, who manage the Assistant Buyers and govern a group of brands. As an employee reaches higher levels in the team, his or her responsibility shifts more from buying activities to mentoring, training, and building the team. This is a core characteristic of Zappos' structure. The company strives to empower employees from the bottom up so that when they are hired as an entry-level employee, within five to seven years they have the opportunity to move up to leadership positions. The top-level positions on this team are the Lead Buyers, who manage the largest one or two brands on the team or on the company's website, and the Director, who rarely ever buys and only mentors and manages.

Because Zappos is an online company, most of the communication that occurs is via e-mail. However in order to ensure that teams function properly and work to reinforce their strong organizational culture, the company encourages face-to-face meetings. Formal meetings between the directors and the various levels on their teams will occur once per month. CEO Tony Hsieh also calls for directors to spend 20 percent of their time with their teams outside of work and gives them an allowance of $50 per month in order to do this. These kinds of activities strengthen the teams by making them more invested in collaboration and instilling trust among team members, as well as with other teams outside of their specific functional area. This serves as a valuable relationship building activity that allows entry-level employees to engage with all levels of the company in a casual manner, promotes brainstorming that results in creative solutions to challenges the team might be facing, and offers all employees a different perspective of their team members and the company they work for.

The most recent development the company has made in terms of organizational structure and teamwork is the adoption of Holacracy. This is a management structure that focuses on the type and amount of work that needs to be accomplished rather than on titles and hierarchy. This seems to be a natural transition for a company whose structure is highlighted by the use of teams and was instituted to avoid rigid structure that leads to inflexibility. The effects of this emerging management style are not fully known; however, it leaves Zappos with an opportunity to show others how it can be successful.[37]

Discussion Questions

1. Why do companies like Zappos incorporate the use of teams into their organizational structure?
2. How does the use of teams contribute to the organizational culture?
3. How does a focus on the work to be accomplished versus the institution of titles relate to the concept of teamwork?

You can find the related video in the Video Library in Connect. Ask your instructor how you can access Connect.

Team Exercise

Assign the responsibility of providing the organizational structure for a company one of your team members has worked for. Was your organization centralized or decentralized in terms of decision making? Would you consider the span of control to be wide or narrow? Were any types of teams, committees, or task forces utilized in the organization? Report your work to the class.

3

Managing Human Resources
人力资源管理

Learning Objectives

After reading this chapter, you will be able to:

LO 3-1 Define human resources management, and explain its significance.

LO 3-2 Summarize the processes of recruiting and selecting human resources for a company.

LO 3-3 Discuss how workers are trained and their performance appraised.

LO 3-4 Identify the types of turnover companies may experience, and explain why turnover is an important issue.

LO 3-5 Specify the various ways a worker may be compensated.

LO 3-6 Discuss some of the issues associated with unionized employees, including collective bargaining and dispute resolution.

LO 3-7 Describe the importance of diversity in the workforce.

LO 3-8 Assess an organization's efforts to reduce its workforce size and manage the resulting effects.

Chapter Outline

进入商业世界
Enter the World of Business

太阳马戏团的招聘流程
The Recruitment Process of Cirque du Soleil

Cirque du Soleil is known for its fanciful shows and for being the only circus that does not use animals. It uses a blend of circus arts and street entertainment to entertain guests. This unique organization requires a unique hiring process. The company holds recruiting events on different continents to recruit the best talent. Yet, the hiring process is based on the creative capacity of applicants more than their current skills or past experience. People from various ethnic backgrounds and professional careers submit their applications through different categories called pools. Recruiters go through these pools to find the applicants they think will be a good fit for the company. About one-third of new hires come from these pools.

Cirque du Soleil requires the recruiter to look not only at skills and accomplishments, but also to foresee what the applicant could become if chosen to be part of the team. Transformation, creativity, and openness are crucial to the success of Cirque du Soleil productions and must be manifested in potential performers. Interviewers will often ask unusual questions to see what kinds of creative responses they get. The diversity of applicants requires that recruiters are sensitive to various ways of interacting with potential employees. For example, some applicants are athletes who are contracted with their government, some are from circus families, and others are represented through agencies. Cirque du Soleil attracts a number of people with unique talents, from athletic skills to pick-pocketing as a part of the show. In each of these instances, there are different protocols and customs that must be observed. While looking for people with skill sets of high quality, the recruiters must also make sure that the applicants are open to becoming a true performer.[1]

引言
Introduction

If a business is to achieve success, it must have sufficient numbers of employees who are qualified and motivated to perform the required duties. Thus, managing the quantity (from hiring to firing) and quality (through training, compensating, and so on) of employees is an important business function. Meeting the challenge of managing increasingly diverse human resources effectively can give a company a competitive edge in a global marketplace.

人力资源管理
human resources management (HRM)
all the activities involved in determining an organization's human resources needs, as well as acquiring, training, and compensating people to fill those needs

This chapter focuses on the quantity and quality of human resources. First we look at how human resources managers plan for, recruit, and select qualified employees. Next we look at training, appraising, and compensating employees, aspects of human resources management designed to retain valued employees. Along the way, we'll also consider the challenges of managing unionized employees and workplace diversity.

LO 3-1

人力资源管理的本质
The Nature of Human Resources Management

Today's organizations are more diverse, with a greater range of women, minorities, and older workers.

We definds human resources as labor, the physical and mental abilities that people use to produce goods and services. **Human resources management (HRM)** refers to all the activities involved in determining an organization's human resources needs, as well as acquiring, training, and compensating people to fill those needs. Human resources managers are concerned with maximizing the satisfaction of employees and motivating them to meet organizational objectives productively. In some companies, this function is called personnel management.

HRM has increased in importance over the past few decades, in part because managers have developed a better understanding of human relations through the work of Maslow, Herzberg, and others. Moreover, the human resources themselves are changing. Employees today are concerned not only about how much a job pays; they are concerned also with job satisfaction, personal performance, recreation, benefits, the work environment, and their opportunities for advancement. Once dominated by white men, today's workforce includes significantly more women, African Americans, Hispanics, and other minorities, as well as disabled and older workers. Human resources managers must be aware of these changes and leverage them to increase the productivity of their employees. Every manager practices some of the functions of human resources management at all times.

人力资源需求规划
Planning for Human Resources Needs

connect

Need help understanding the Five Steps of Human Resource Planning? Visit your Connect ebook video tab for a brief animated explanation.

When planning and developing strategies for reaching the organization's overall objectives, a company must consider whether it will have the human resources necessary to carry out its plans. After determining how many employees and what skills are needed to satisfy the overall plans, the human resources department (which may range from the owner in a small business to hundreds of people in a large corporation) ascertains how many employees the company currently has and how many will be retiring or otherwise leaving the organization during the planning period. With this information, the human resources manager can then forecast how many more employees the company will need to hire and what qualifications they must have, or determine if layoffs are required to meet demand more efficiently. HRM planning also requires forecasting the availability of people in the workforce who will have the necessary qualifications to meet the organization's future needs. The human resources manager then develops a strategy for satisfying the organization's human resources needs. As organizations strive to increase efficiency through outsourcing, automation, or learning to effectively use temporary workers, hiring needs can change dramatically.

Next, managers analyze the jobs within the organization so that they can match the human resources to the available assignments. **Job analysis** determines, through observation and study, pertinent information about a job—the specific tasks that comprise it; the knowledge, skills, and abilities necessary to perform it; and the environment in which it will be performed. Managers use the information obtained through a job analysis to develop job descriptions and job specifications.

岗位分析
job analysis
the determination, through observation and study, of pertinent information about a job—including specific tasks and necessary abilities, knowledge, and skills

A **job description** is a formal, written explanation of a specific job that usually includes job title, tasks to be performed (for instance, waiting on customers), relationship with other jobs, physical and mental skills required (such as lifting heavy boxes or calculating data), duties, responsibilities, and working conditions. Job seekers might turn to online websites or databases to help find job descriptions for specific occupations. For instance, the Occupational Information Network has an online database with hundreds of occupational descriptors. These descriptors describe the skills, knowledge, and education needed to fulfill a particular occupation (e.g., human resources).[2] A **job specification** describes the qualifications necessary for a specific job, in terms of education (some jobs require a college degree), experience, personal characteristics (ads frequently request outgoing, hardworking persons), and physical characteristics. Both the job description and job specification are used to develop recruiting materials such as newspapers, trade publications, and online advertisements.

职位描述
job description
a formal, written explanation of a specific job, usually including job title, tasks, relationship with other jobs, physical and mental skills required, duties, responsibilities, and working conditions

职位说明
job specification
a description of the qualifications necessary for a specific job, in terms of education, experience, and personal and physical characteristics

招聘和甄选新员工
Recruiting and Selecting New Employees

LO 3-2

After forecasting the firm's human resources needs and comparing them to existing human resources, the human resources manager should have a general idea of how many new employees the firm needs to hire. With the aid of job analyses, management can then recruit and select employees who are qualified to fill specific job openings.

招聘
Recruiting

Recruiting means forming a pool of qualified applicants from which management can select employees. There are two sources from which to develop this pool of applicants—internal and external.

招聘
recruiting
forming a pool of qualified applicants from which management can select employees

Internal sources of applicants include the organization's current employees. Many firms have a policy of giving first consideration to their own employees—or promoting from within. The cost of hiring current employees to fill job openings is inexpensive when compared with the cost of hiring from external sources, and it is good for employee morale. However, hiring from within creates another job vacancy to be filled.

External sources of applicants consist of advertisements in newspapers and professional journals, employment agencies, colleges, vocational schools, recommendations from current employees, competing firms, unsolicited applications, online websites, and social networking sites such as LinkedIn. Internships are also a good way to solicit for potential employees. Many companies hire college students or recent graduates to low-paying internships that give them the opportunity to get hands-on experience on the job. If the intern proves to be a good fit, an organization may

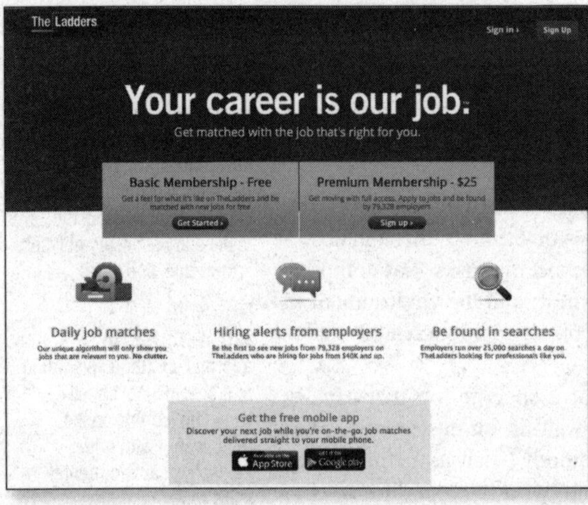

TheLadders.com is a website that targets career-driven professionals.

then hire the intern as a full-time worker. There are also hundreds of websites where employers can post job openings and job seekers can post their résumés, including Monster.com, USAJobs, Simply Hired, SnagaJob, and CareerBuilder.com. TheLadders.com is a website that focuses on career-driven professionals who make salaries of $40,000 or more. Employers looking for employees for specialized jobs can use more focused sites such as computerwork.com. Increasingly, companies can turn to their own websites for potential candidates: Nearly all of the *Fortune* 500 firms provide career websites where they recruit, provide employment information, and take applications. Using these sources of applicants is generally more expensive than hiring from within, but it may be necessary if there are no current employees who meet the job specifications or there are better-qualified people outside of the organization. Recruiting for entry-level managerial and professional positions is often carried out on college and university campuses. For managerial or professional positions above the entry level, companies sometimes depend on employment agencies or executive search firms, sometimes called *headhunters,* which specialize in luring qualified people away from other companies. Employers are also increasingly using professional social networking sites such as LinkedIn and Viadeo as recruitment tools. Figure 3.1 shows some ways that recruiters use social media to recruit and hire job candidates.

FIGURE 3.1
Recruiting through Social Networking

Online survey conducted June 2013 with 1,600 recruiting and human resources professionals.

Source: Jobvite, *Social Survey Recruiting Results 2013.*

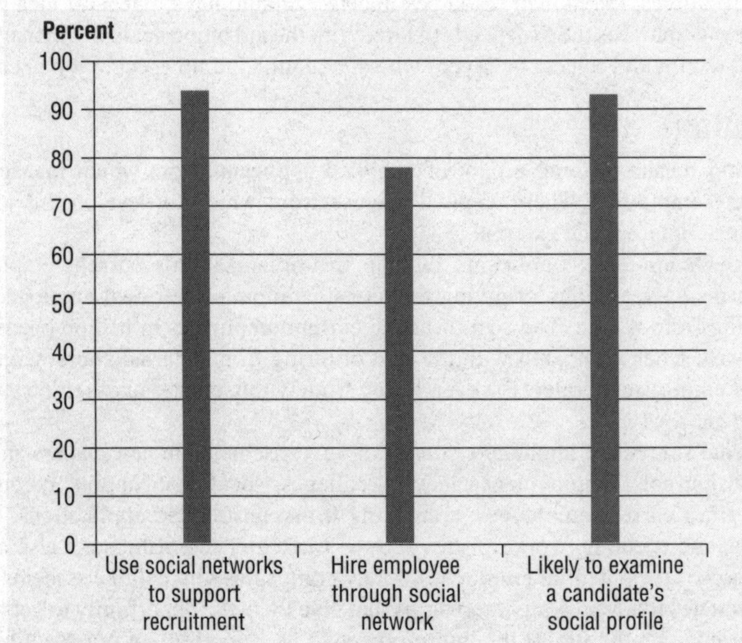

甄选
Selection

甄选
selection
the process of collecting information about applicants and using that information to make hiring decisions

Selection is the process of collecting information about applicants and using that information to decide which ones to hire. It includes the application itself, as well as interviewing, testing, and reference checking. This process can be quite lengthy and expensive. Procter & Gamble, for example, offers online applications for jobs in approximately 100 countries. The first round of evaluation involves assessment, and if this stage goes well, the candidate interviews in the region or country to which the applicant applied.[3] Such rigorous scrutiny is necessary to find those applicants who can do the work expected and fit into the firm's structure and culture. If an organization finds the "right" employees through its recruiting and selection process, it will not have to spend as much money later in recruiting, selecting, and training replacement employees.

申请

The Application. In the first stage of the selection process, the individual fills out an application form and perhaps has a brief interview. The application form asks for the applicant's name, address, telephone number, education, and previous work experience. The goal of this stage of the selection process is to get acquainted with the applicants and to weed out those who are obviously not qualified for the job. For employees with work experience, most companies ask for the following information before contacting a potential candidate: current salary, reason for seeking a new job, years of experience, availability, and level of interest in the position. In addition to identifying obvious qualifications, the application can provide subtle clues about whether a person is appropriate for a particular job. For instance, an applicant who gives unusually creative answers may be perfect for a position at an advertising agency; a person who turns in a sloppy, hurriedly scrawled application probably would not be appropriate for a technical job requiring precise adjustments. Most companies now accept online applications. The online application for Target is designed not only to collect biographical data on the applicant, but also to create a picture of the applicant and how that person might contribute to the company. The completion of the survey takes about 15–45 minutes, depending on the position. To get a better view of the fit between the applicant and the company, the online application contains a questionnaire that asks applicants more specific questions, from how they might react in a certain situation to personality attributes like self-esteem or ability to interact with people.

面试

The Interview. The next phase of the selection process involves interviewing applicants. Table 3.1 provides some insights on finding the right work environment. Interviews allow management to obtain detailed information about the applicant's experience and skills, reasons for changing jobs, attitudes toward the job, and an idea of whether the person would fit in with the company. Table 3.2 lists some of the most common questions asked by interviewers while Table 3.3 reveals some common

TABLE 3.1
Interviewing Tips

1. Evaluate the work environment. Do employees seem to get along and work well in teams?
2. Evaluate the attitude of employees. Are employees happy, tense, or overworked?
3. Are employees enthusiastic and excited about their work?
4. What is the organizational culture, and would you feel comfortable working there?

Source: Adapted from "What to Look for During Office Visits".

TABLE 3.2
Most Common Questions Asked during the Interview

1. Tell me about yourself.
2. Why should I hire you?
3. Please tell me about your future objectives.
4. Has your education prepared you for your career?
5. Have you been a team player?
6. Did you encounter any conflict with your previous professors or employer? What are the steps that you have taken to resolve this issue?
7. What is your biggest weakness?
8. How would your professors describe you?
9. What are the qualities that a manager should possess?
10. If you could turn back time, what would you change?

Source: "Job Interview Skills Training: Top Ten Interview Questions for College Graduates," February 17, 2010.

TABLE 3.3
Mistakes Made in Interviewing

1. Not taking the interview seriously.
2. Not dressing appropriately (dressing down).
3. Not appropriately discussing experience, abilities, and education.
4. Being too modest about your accomplishments.
5. Talking too much.
6. Too much concern about compensation.
7. Speaking negatively of a former employer.
8. Not asking enough or appropriate questions.
9. Not showing the proper enthusiasm level.
10. Not engaging in appropriate follow-up to the interview.

Source: "Avoid the Top 10 Job Interview Mistakes," All Business.

mistakes candidates make in interviewing. Furthermore, the interviewer can answer the applicant's questions about the requirements for the job, compensation, working conditions, company policies, organizational culture, and so on. A potential employee's questions may be just as revealing as his or her answers. Today's students might be surprised to have an interviewer ask them, "What's on your Facebook account?" or have them show the interviewer their Facebook accounts. Currently, these are legal questions for an interviewer to ask.

测试

Testing. Another step in the selection process is testing. Ability and performance tests are used to determine whether an applicant has the skills necessary for the job.

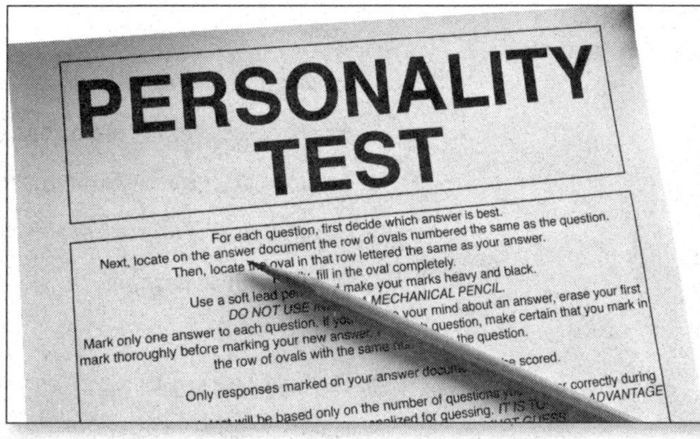

Personality tests such as Myers-Briggs are used to assess an applicant's potential for a certain kind of job. For instance, extroversion and a love of people would be good qualities for a retail job.

Aptitude, IQ, or personality tests may be used to assess an applicant's potential for a certain kind of work and his or her ability to fit into the organization's culture. One of the most commonly used tests is the Myers-Briggs Type Indicator. The Myers-Briggs Type Indicator Test is used worldwide by millions of people each year. Although polygraph ("lie detector") tests were once a common technique for evaluating the honesty of applicants, in 1988 their use was restricted to specific government jobs and those involving security or access to drugs. Applicants may also undergo physical examinations to determine their suitability for some jobs, and many companies require applicants to be screened for illegal drug use. Illegal drug use and alcoholism can be particularly damaging to businesses. It has been estimated that 8.4 percent of full-time employees engage in illicit drug use, while 29.7 percent engage in binge drinking and 8.5 percent are considered to be heavy drinkers.[4] Small businesses may have a higher percentage of these employees because they do not engage in systematic drug testing. If you employ a drug or alcohol abuser, you can expect a 33 percent loss in productivity from this employee. Loss in productivity from alcohol abuse alone costs companies $134 billion each year. Health care costs are also more expensive for those who abuse alcohol—twice as more than those for employees who do not abuse alcohol.[5]

Because computer knowledge is a requirement for many jobs today, certain companies also require an applicant to take a typing test or tests to determine their knowledge of MS Word, Excel, PowerPoint, and/or other necessary programs. Like the application form and the interview, testing serves to eliminate those who do not meet the job specifications.

背景调查

Reference Checking. Before making a job offer, the company should always check an applicant's references. Reference checking usually involves verifying educational background and previous work experience. An Internet search is often done to determine social media activities or other public activities. While public Internet searches are usually deemed acceptable, asking for private information—while legal—is deemed to be intrusive by many job seekers.[6] Many states are already taking legislative action to ban this practice.[7] Public companies are likely to do more extensive background searches to make sure applicants are not misrepresenting themselves.

Background checking is important because applicants may misrepresent themselves on their applications or résumés. Matthew Martoma, a trader for SAC Capital Advisors, was convicted of conspiracy and securities fraud. Court testimony revealed that he had been expelled from Harvard after forging a transcript for an application and creating an elaborate cover-up. Research has shown that those who are willing to exaggerate or lie on their résumés are more likely to engage in unethical behaviors.[8] As Table 3.4 illustrates, some of the most common types of résumé lies include the faking of credentials, overstatements of skills or accomplishments, lies concerning education/degrees, omissions of past employment, and the falsification of references.[9]

TABLE 3.4
Top 10 Résumé Lies

1. Stretching dates of employment
2. Inflating past accomplishments and skills
3. Enhancing job titles and responsibilities
4. Education exaggeration and fabricating degrees
5. Unexplained gaps and periods of “self employment”
6. Omitting past employment
7. Faking credentials
8. Fabricating reasons for leaving previous job
9. Providing fraudulent references
10. Misrepresenting military record

Source: Christopher T. Marquet and Lisa J. B. Peterson, “Résumé Fraud: The Top 10 Lies”.

Reference checking is a vital, albeit often overlooked, stage in the selection process. Managers charged with hiring should be aware, however, that many organizations will confirm only that an applicant is a former employee, perhaps with beginning and ending work dates, and will not release details about the quality of the employee’s work.

招聘和甄选中的法律问题
Legal Issues in Recruiting and Selecting

Legal constraints and regulations are present in almost every phase of the recruitment and selection process, and a violation of these regulations can result in lawsuits and fines. Therefore, managers should be aware of these restrictions to avoid legal problems. Some of the laws affecting human resources management are discussed here.

《民权法案》第七章
Title VII of the Civil Rights Act
prohibits discrimination in employment and created the Equal Employment Opportunity Commission

Because one law pervades all areas of human resources management, we’ll take a quick look at it now. **Title VII of the Civil Rights Act** of 1964 prohibits discrimination in employment. It also created the Equal Employment Opportunity Commission (EEOC), a federal agency dedicated to increasing job opportunities for women and minorities and eliminating job discrimination based on race, religion, color, sex, national origin, or handicap. As a result of Title VII, employers must not impose sex distinctions in job specifications, job descriptions, or newspaper advertisements. In 2013, workplace discrimination charges filed with the EEOC were 93,727. The EEOC received more than 7,200 charges of sexual harassment. Sexual harassment often makes up the largest number of claims the EEOC encounters each day.[10] The Civil Rights Act of 1964 also outlaws the use of discriminatory tests for applicants. Aptitude tests and other indirect tests must be validated; in other words, employers must be able to demonstrate that scores on such tests are related to job performance, so that no one race has an advantage in taking the tests or is alternatively discriminated against. Although many hope for improvements in organizational diversity, only 4.4 percent of *Fortune* 500 companies are run by people of color. Despite the low number, this is an improvement from the mid-1990s when no *Fortune* 500 company had a person of color as a CEO. Additionally, 13.3 percent of board seats are now held by racial minorities.[11]

Title VII of the Civil Rights Act prohibits discrimination in employment. People who feel they have been discriminated against can file a formal complaint with the Equal Employment Opportunity Commission.

Other laws affecting HRM include the Americans with Disabilities Act (ADA), which prevents discrimination against disabled persons. It also classifies people with AIDS as handicapped and, consequently, prohibits using a positive AIDS test as reason to deny an applicant employment. The Age Discrimination in Employment Act specifically outlaws discrimination based on age. Its focus is banning hiring practices that discriminate against people 40 years and older. Generally, when companies need employees, recruiters head to college campuses, and when downsizing is necessary, many older workers are offered early retirement. Forced retirement based on age, however, is generally considered to be illegal in the United States, although claims of forced retirement still abound. Until recently, employees in the United Kingdom could be forced to retire at age 65. However, a new law abolished the default retirement age.[12] Indeed there are many benefits that companies are realizing in hiring older workers. Some of these benefits include the fact that they are more dedicated, punctual, honest, and detail-oriented; are good listeners; take pride in their work; exhibit good organizational skills; are efficient and confident; are mature; can be seen as role models; have good communication skills; and offer an opportunity for a reduced labor cost because of already having insurance plans.[13] Figure 3.2 shows the age ranges of employed workers in the United States.

The Equal Pay Act mandates that men and women who do equal work must receive the same wage. Wage differences are acceptable only if they are attributed to seniority, performance, or qualifications. In the United States, the typical full-time female employee earns 17.2 percent less than the average full-time employee.[14] In a study by PayScale, gender pay gaps can be found in positions such as chief executive (women earn 87 percent of what men earn), software architect (women earn 88 percent of what men earn), and executive chef (women earn 91 percent of what men earn).[15] Performance quality in these jobs is relatively subjective. Jobs like engineers, actuaries, or electricians, where the performance evaluation is more objective, result in greater salary parity between men and women.[16] However, despite the wage inequalities that still exist, women in the workplace are becoming increasingly accepted among both genders. The working mother is no longer a novelty; in fact, many working mothers seek the same amount of achievement as working men and women who are not mothers.

FIGURE 3.2
U.S. Population Employed by Age Group (in thousands)

Source: Bureau of Labor Statistics, labor force statistics from the *Current Population Survey.*

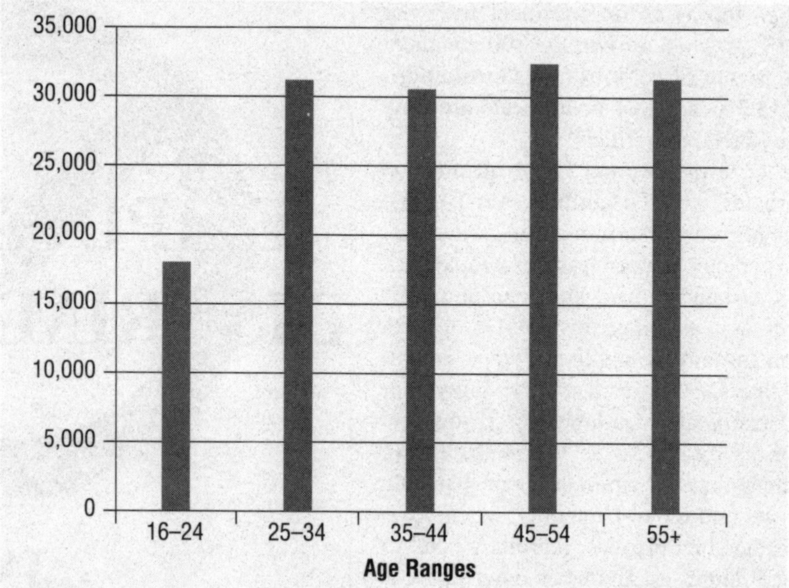

员工培养
Developing the Workforce

新人引导
orientation
familiarizing newly hired employees with fellow workers, company procedures, and the physical properties of the company

Once the most qualified applicants have been selected, have been offered positions, and have accepted their offers, they must be formally introduced to the organization and trained so they can begin to be productive members of the workforce. **Orientation** familiarizes the newly hired employees with fellow workers, company procedures, and the physical properties of the company. It generally includes a tour of the building; introductions to supervisors, co-workers, and subordinates; and the distribution of organizational manuals describing the organization's policy on vacations, absenteeism, lunch breaks, company benefits, and so on. Orientation also involves socializing the new employee into the ethics and culture of the new company. Many larger companies now show videotapes of procedures, facilities, and key personnel in the organization to help speed the adjustment process.

员工培训与发展
Training and Development

LO 3-3

培训
training
teaching employees to do specific job tasks through either classroom development or on-the-job experience

发展
development
training that augments the skills and knowledge of managers and professionals

Although recruiting and selection are designed to find employees who have the knowledge, skills, and abilities the company needs, new employees still must undergo **training** to learn how to do their specific job tasks. *On-the-job training* allows workers to learn by actually performing the tasks of the job, while *classroom training* teaches employees with lectures, conferences, videotapes, case studies, and web-based training. For instance, McDonald's trains those interested in company operations and leadership development at the Fred L. Turner Training Center, otherwise known as Hamburger University. Hamburger University employs full-time professors to train students in a variety of topics, including crew development, restaurant management, middle management, and executive development. Training includes classroom instruction, hands-on instruction, and computer e-learning.[17] **Development** is training that augments the skills and knowledge of managers and professionals. Training and development are also used to improve the skills of employees in their present positions and to prepare them for increased responsibility and job promotions. Training is therefore a vital function of human resources management. At the Container Store, for example, first-year sales personnel receive 263 hours of training about the company's products.[18] Companies are engaging in more experiential and involvement-oriented training exercises for employees. Use of role-plays, simulations, and online training methods are becoming increasingly popular in employee training.

McDonald's has expanded its famous Hamburger University into China. This branch of Hamburger University will train a new generation of Chinese students in such areas as restaurant management, leadership development, and other skills.

绩效评估
Assessing Performance

Assessing an employee's performance—his or her strengths and weaknesses on the job—is one of the most difficult tasks for managers. However, performance appraisal is crucial because it gives employees feedback on how they are doing and what they need to do to improve. It also provides a basis for determining how to compensate and reward employees, and it generates information about the quality of the firm's selection, training, and development activities. Table 3.5 identifies 16 characteristics that may be assessed in a performance review.

TABLE 3.5
Performance Characteristics

• **Productivity**—rate at which work is regularly produced
• **Quality**—accuracy, professionalism, and deliverability of produced work
• **Job knowledge**—understanding of the objectives, practices, and standards of work
• **Problem solving**—ability to identify and correct problems effectively
• **Communication**—effectiveness in written and verbal exchanges
• **Initiative**—willingness to identify and address opportunities for improvement
• **Adaptability**—ability to become comfortable with change
• **Planning and organization skills**—reflected through the ability to schedule projects, set goals, and maintain organizational systems
• **Teamwork and cooperation**—effectiveness of collaborations with co-workers
• **Judgment**—ability to determine appropriate actions in a timely manner
• **Dependability**—responsiveness, reliability, and conscientiousness demonstrated on the job
• **Creativity**—extent to which resourceful ideas, solutions, and methods for task completion are proposed
• **Sales**—demonstrated through success in selling products, services, yourself, and your company
• **Customer service**—ability to communicate effectively with customers, address problems, and offer solutions that meet or exceed their expectations
• **Leadership**—tendency and ability to serve as a doer, guide, decision maker, and role model
• **Financial management**—appropriateness of cost controls and financial planning within the scope defined by the position

Performance appraisals are important because they provide employees with feedback on how well they are doing as well as areas for improvement.

Performance appraisals may be objective or subjective. An objective assessment is quantifiable. For example, a Westinghouse employee might be judged by how many circuit boards he typically produces in one day or by how many of his boards have defects. A Century 21 real estate agent might be judged by the number of houses she has shown or the number of sales she has closed. A company can also use tests as an objective method of assessment. Whatever method they use, managers must take into account the work environment when they appraise performance objectively.

When jobs do not lend themselves to objective appraisal, the manager must relate the employee's performance to some other standard. One popular tool used in subjective assessment is the ranking system, which lists various performance factors on which the manager ranks employees against each other. Although used by many large companies, ranking systems are unpopular with many employees. Qualitative criteria, such as teamwork and communication skills, used to evaluate employees are generally hard to gauge. Such grading systems have triggered employee lawsuits that allege discrimination in grade/ranking assignments. For example, one manager may grade a company's employees one way, while another manager grades a group more harshly depending on the managers' grading style. If layoffs occur, then employees graded by the second manager may be more likely to lose their jobs. Other criticisms of grading systems include unclear wording or inappropriate words that a manager may unintentionally write in a performance evaluation, like *young* or *pretty* to describe an employee's appearance. These liabilities can all be fodder for lawsuits should employees allege that they were treated unfairly. It is therefore crucial that managers use clear language in performance evaluations and be consistent with all employees. Several employee grading computer packages have been developed to make performance evaluations easier for managers and clearer for employees.[19] Figure 3.3 demonstrates that employers are more likely to believe that performance reviews improve employee performance than employees do.

FIGURE 3.3 Performance Reviews: Those Who Believe Reviews Improve Employees' Performance

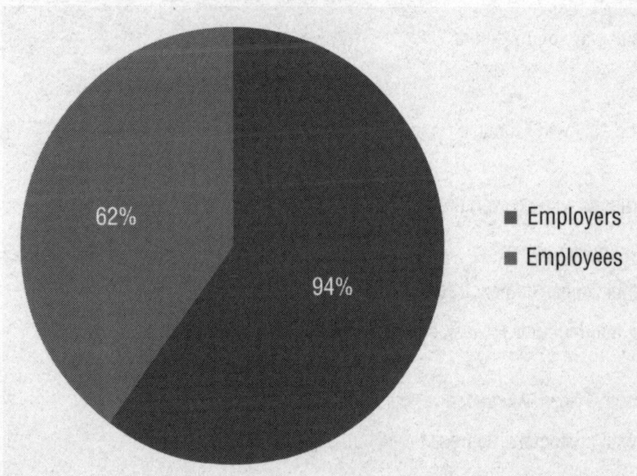

Robert Half survey of 1,400 chief financial officers and 422 workers, 2012. Survey developed by Accountemps.

Source: Accountemps, "Mixed Review for the Employee Review," July 12, 2012.

Another performance appraisal method used by many companies is the 360-degree feedback system, which provides feedback from a panel that typically includes superiors, peers, and subordinates. Because of the tensions it may cause, peer appraisal appears to be difficult for many. However, companies that have success with 360-degree feedback tend to be open to learning and willing to experiment and are led by executives who are direct about the expected benefits as well as the challenges.[20] Managers and leaders with a high emotional intelligence (sensitivity to their own as well as others' emotions) assess and reflect upon their interactions with colleagues on a daily basis. In addition, they conduct follow-up analysis on their projects, asking the right questions and listening carefully to responses without getting defensive of their actions.[21]

Whether the assessment is objective or subjective, it is vital that the manager discuss the results with the employee, so that the employee knows how well he or she is doing the job. The results of a performance appraisal become useful only when they are communicated, tactfully, to the employee and presented as a tool to allow the employee to grow and improve in his or her position and beyond. Performance appraisals are also used to determine whether an employee should be promoted, transferred, or terminated from the organization.

人员流动
turnover
occurs when employees quit or are fired and must be replaced by new employees

人员流动
Turnover

LO 3-4

Turnover, which occurs when employees quit or are fired and must be replaced by new employees, results in lost productivity from the vacancy, costs to recruit replacement employees, management time devoted to interviewing, training, and socialization expenses for new employees. However, some companies have created innovative solutions for reducing turnover. Accenture, a global management consulting firm, has 275,000 employees around the world who travel frequently. Because of the hectic pace of the job and constant traveling, the company has instituted a unique wellness program offered to its on-the-go employees to encourage them to take care of their health while getting their jobs done. This program is personalized to the lifestyles of the employees and offers health tips and exercises that are effective but not time consuming. Accenture employees have rated this program as fun and relevant to their lives, resulting in higher job satisfaction. Job satisfaction is one of the best ways of reducing turnover.[22] Part of the reason for turnover may be overworked employees as a result of downsizing and a lack of training and advancement opportunities.[23] Of course, turnover is not always an unhappy occasion when it takes the form of a promotion or transfer.

晋升
promotion
an advancement to a higher-level job with increased authority, responsibility, and pay

调岗
transfer
a move to another job within the company at essentially the same level and wage

离职
separations
employment changes involving resignation, retirement, termination, or layoff

A **promotion** is an advancement to a higher-level job with increased authority, responsibility, and pay. In some companies and most labor unions, seniority—the length of time a person has been with the company or at a particular job classification—is the key issue in determining who should be promoted. Most managers base promotions on seniority only when they have candidates with equal qualifications: Managers prefer to base promotions on merit.

A **transfer** is a move to another job within the company at essentially the same level and wage. Transfers allow workers to obtain new skills or to find a new position within an organization when their old position has been eliminated because of automation or downsizing.

Separations occur when employees resign, retire, are terminated, or are laid off. Employees may be terminated, or fired, for poor performance, violation of work rules, absenteeism, and so on. Businesses have traditionally been able to fire employees *at will,* that is, for any reason other than for race, religion, sex, or age, or because an employee is a union organizer. However, recent legislation and court decisions now require that companies fire employees fairly, for just cause only. Managers must take care, then, to warn employees when their performance is unacceptable and may lead to dismissal, elevating the importance of performance evaluations. They should also document all problems and warnings in employees' work records. To avoid the possibility of lawsuits from individuals who may feel they

Many companies in recent years are choosing to downsize by eliminating jobs. Reasons for downsizing might be due to financial constraints or the need to become more productive and competitive.

TABLE 3.6
What You Should Not Do When You Are Terminated

1. Do not tell off your boss and co-workers, even if you think they deserve it.
2. Do not damage company property or steal something.
3. Do not forget to ask for a reference.
4. Do not badmouth your employer or any of your co-workers to your replacement.
5. Do not badmouth your employer to a prospective employer when you go on a job interview.

Source: Dawn Rosenberg McKay, "Five Things Not to Do When You Leave Your Job".

have been fired unfairly, employers should provide clear, business-related reasons for any firing, supported by written documentation if possible. Employee disciplinary procedures should be carefully explained to all employees and should be set forth in employee handbooks. Table 3.6 illustrates what *not* to do when you are terminated.

Many companies have downsized in recent years, laying off tens of thousands of employees in their effort to become more productive and competitive. For example, Radio Shack had to lay off workers after it decided to close more than 1,000 stores in the United State. The electronics retailer suffered declining sales as consumers increasingly purchase such items online.[24] Layoffs are sometimes temporary; employees may be brought back when business conditions improve. When layoffs are to be permanent, employers often help employees find other jobs and may extend benefits while the employees search for new employment. Such actions help lessen the trauma of the layoffs. Fortunately, there are several business areas that are choosing not to downsize.

A well-organized human resources department strives to minimize losses due to separations and transfers because recruiting and training new employees is very expensive. Note that a high turnover rate in a company may signal problems with the selection and training process, the compensation program, or even the type of company. To help reduce turnover, companies have tried a number of strategies, including giving employees more interesting job responsibilities (job enrichment), allowing for increased job flexibility, and providing more employee benefits.

员工薪酬
Compensating the Workforce

LO 3-5

People generally don't work for free, and how much they are paid for their work is a complicated issue. Also, designing a fair compensation plan is an important task because pay and benefits represent a substantial portion of an organization's expenses. Wages that are too high may result in the company's products being priced too high, making them uncompetitive in the market. Wages that are too low may damage employee morale and result in costly turnover. Remember that compensation is one of the hygiene factors identified by Herzberg.

Designing a fair compensation plan is a difficult task because it involves evaluating the relative worth of all jobs within the business while allowing for individual efforts. Compensation for a specific job is typically determined through a **wage/salary survey,** which tells the company how much compensation comparable firms are paying for specific jobs that the firms have in common. Compensation for individuals within a specific job category depends on both the compensation for that job and the individual's productivity. Therefore, two employees with identical jobs may not receive exactly the same pay because of individual differences in performance.

薪资调查
wage/salary survey
a study that tells a company how much compensation comparable firms are paying for specific jobs that the firms have in common

Going Green

Sustainability Job Opportunities

As businesses become more focused on their environmental impact, job opportunities in sustainability are increasing. These positions, while present in some small businesses, are more common in larger organizations that use a lot of energy and generally have a larger impact on the environment. They exist in both the public and private sectors. Because these positions are becoming more important, sometimes employees—if savvy and persuasive enough—can create a sustainability position or department within the companies at which they currently work.

Some positions in this field require strong leadership and communication skills over technical knowledge in sustainability practices. People in this area generally create an atmosphere of sustainability as an institutional goal, bring employees and departments together to define and meet short-term goals, ensure communication channels around sustainability are open, and compile sustainability reports.

Other positions require knowledge in life-cycle and supply chain operations and management. These people are generally inclined toward more quantitative responsibilities in engineering, finance, and technical project management and support the activities of energy systems and building maintenance requirements. Finally, sustainability positions can be found in planning and design. Employees in these positions engage in the development of transportation avenues, protection of forests and open spaces, and the incorporation of green attributes to new and existing structures.[25]

Discussion Questions

1. Why are sustainability job opportunities increasing in the business field?
2. Why might a large organization want to adopt a sustainability position or department?
3. Describe the responsibilities for different jobs in sustainability.

经济报酬
Financial Compensation

工资
wages
financial rewards based on the number of hours the employee works or the level of output achieved

Financial compensation falls into two general categories—wages and salaries. **Wages** are financial rewards based on the number of hours the employee works or the level of output achieved. Wages based on the number of hours worked are called time wages. The federal minimum wage increased to \$7.25 per hour in 2009 for covered nonexempt workers.[26] However, Congress is expected to vote on whether to increase the minimum wage to \$10.10. If passed, the minimum wage would increase over the next few years. Many members of Congress want to increase the minimum wage to \$15 per hour.[27] Tipped wages must be \$2.13 per hour as long as tips plus the wage of \$2.13 per hour equal the minimum wage of \$7.25 per hour.[28] Many states also mandate minimum wages; in the case where the two wages are in conflict, the higher of the two wages prevails. There may even be differences between city and state minimum wages. In New Mexico, the minimum wage is \$7.50, whereas in the state capitol of Santa Fe, the minimum wage is \$10.66, due to a higher cost of living. When Santa Fe went to \$10.66 per hour on March 1, 2014, this became the third highest minimum wage in the United States after Seattle-Tacoma, Washington, at \$15 per hour and San Francisco at \$10.74 per hour.[29] Table 3.7 compares wages and other information for Costco and Walmart, two well-known discount chains. Time wages are appropriate when employees are continually interrupted and when quality is more important than quantity. Assembly-line workers, clerks, and maintenance personnel are commonly paid on a time-wage basis. The advantage of time wages is the ease of computation. The disadvantage is that time wages provide no incentive to increase productivity. In fact, time wages may encourage employees to be less productive.

To overcome these disadvantages, many companies pay on an incentive system, using piece wages or commissions. Piece wages are based on the level of output achieved. A major advantage of piece wages is that they motivate employees to

TABLE 3.7
Costco versus Walmart

	Costco	Walmart
Number of employees	185,000+	2,200,000
Revenues	$99.1 billion	$469.2 billion
Average pay per hour	$21	$12.83
World's most admired ranking	12	28
Strengths	Management quality; financial soundness; people management	Management quality; financial soundness; global competitiveness

Sources: "Fortune Global 500," CNN Money, *2014; "Fortune World's Most Admired Rankings,"* CNN Money, *2014; Costco Wholesale, "Investor Relations"; Kevin Short, "11 Reasons to Love Costco That Have Nothing to Do with Shopping,"* Huffington Post, *November 19, 2013; "Wal-Mart,"* NY JobSource, *January 26, 2014.*

supervise their own activities and to increase output. Skilled craftworkers are often paid on a piece-wage basis.

提成
commission
an incentive system that pays a fixed amount or a percentage of the employee's sales

The other incentive system, **commission,** pays a fixed amount or a percentage of the employee's sales. Kele & Co Jewelers in Plainfield, Illinois, make sterling silver jewelry and offer semi-precious stones and gemstones at affordable prices. Their handcrafted jewelry is sold through the Internet and through independent sales representatives (ISRs) all over the country. The unique sdpect of Kele's sales process is their innovative sales and commission structure. ISRs have no minimum sales quotas, sales are shared among team members during training and after being promoted, and there is no requirement to purchase inventory as jewelry is shipped from Kele headquarters. ISRs receive a 30 to 50 percent commission on sales. The goal is to increase the profit margin and earning potential of the salespeople. The company's goal is to become the largest direct sales company in the industry.[30] This method motivates employees to sell as much as they can. Some companies also combine payment based on commission with time wages or salaries.

薪金
salary
a financial reward calculated on a weekly, monthly, or annual basis

A **salary** is a financial reward calculated on a weekly, monthly, or annual basis. Salaries are associated with white-collar workers such as office personnel, executives, and professional employees. Although a salary provides a stable stream of income, salaried workers may be required to work beyond usual hours without additional financial compensation.

奖金
bonuses
monetary rewards offered by companies for exceptional performance as incentives to further increase productivity

In addition to the basic wages or salaries paid to employees, a company may offer **bonuses** for exceptional performance as an incentive to increase productivity further. Many workers receive a bonus as a "thank you" for good work and an incentive to continue working hard. Many owners and managers are recognizing that simple bonuses and perks foster happier employees and reduce turnover. Bonuses are especially popular among Wall Street firms. In 2014, Wall Street disbursed more than $26 billion in bonuses to more than 165,000 employees. This amount is 15 percent more than the year before and is the third largest bonus sum ever given out.[31]

利润分享
profit sharing
a form of compensation whereby a percentage of company profits is distributed to the employees whose work helped to generate them

Another form of compensation is **profit sharing,** which distributes a percentage of company profits to the employees whose work helped to generate those profits. Some profit-sharing plans involve distributing shares of company stock to employees.

Usually referred to as *ESOPs*—employee stock ownership plans—they have been gaining popularity in recent years. One reason for the popularity of ESOPs is the sense of partnership that they create between the organization and employees. Profit sharing can also motivate employees to work hard, because increased productivity and sales mean that the profits or the stock dividends will increase. Many organizations offer employees a stake in the company through stock purchase plans, ESOPs, or stock investments through 401(k) plans. Employees below senior management levels rarely received stock options until recently. Companies are adopting broad-based stock option plans to build a stronger link between employees' interests and the organization's interests. ESOPs have met with enormous success over the years, and employee-owned stock has even outperformed the stock market during certain periods. Many businesses have found employee stock options a great way to boost productivity and increase morale. As of 2014, there were nearly 12,000 ESOPs in the United States.[32]

福利
Benefits

Benefits are nonfinancial forms of compensation provided to employees, such as pension plans for retirement; health, disability, and life insurance; holidays and paid days off for vacation or illness; credit union membership; health programs; child care; elder care; assistance with adoption; and more. According to the Bureau of Labor Statistics, employer costs for employee compensation for civilian workers in the United States average $29.63 per hour worked. Wages and salaries account for approximately 70.1 percent of those costs, while benefits account for 29.9 percent of the cost. Legally required benefits (Social Security, Medicare, federal and state employment insurance, and workers' compensation) account for 8.2 percent of total compensation.[33] Such benefits increase employee security and, to a certain extent, their morale and motivation.

福利
benefits
nonfinancial forms of compensation provided to employees, such as pension plans, health insurance, paid vacation and holidays, and the like

Table 3.8 lists some of the benefits Internet search engine Google offers its employees. Although health insurance is a common benefit for full-time employees, rising health care costs have forced a growing number of employers to trim this benefit. Even government workers, whose wages and benefits used to be virtually guaranteed safe, have seen reductions in health care and other benefits. Surveys have revealed that with the decrease in benefits comes a decrease in employee loyalty. Only 42 percent of employees say they feel a strong sense of loyalty to their employers. However, more than half of respondents indicated that employee benefits were important in decisions to stay with the company. Benefits are particularly important to younger generations of employees.[34] Starbucks recognizes the importance of how benefits can significantly impact an employee's health and well-being. As a result, it is the only fast-food company to offer its part-time employees health insurance.

An onsite fitness center is just one of the benefits that large companies have begun to offer employees. Such onsite benefits like fitness centers and child care are particularly important for employees who work long hours or who struggle to maintain a healthy work-life balance.

A benefit increasingly offered is the employee assistance program (EAP). Each company's EAP is different, but most offer counseling for and assistance with those employees' personal problems that might hurt

TABLE 3.8
Google's Employees' Benefits

• Health insurance:
– Employee medical insurance
– Dental insurance
– Vision insurance
• Vacation (15 days per year for one–three years' employment; 20 days off for four–five years' employment; 25 days for more than six years' employment)
• Twelve paid holidays/year
• Savings plans
– 401(k) retirement plan, matched by Google
– Flexible spending accounts
• Disability and life insurance
• Employee Assistance Program
• Free lunches and snacks
• Massages, gym membership, hair stylist, fitness class, and bike repair
• Weekly activities
• Maternity leave
• Adoption assistance
• Tuition reimbursement
• Employee referral plan
• Onsite doctor
• Backup child care
• Holiday parties, health fair, credit union, roller hockey, outdoor volleyball court, discounts for local attractions

Source: "Google Benefits".

their job performance if not addressed. The most common counseling services offered include drug- and alcohol-abuse treatment programs, fitness programs, smoking cessation clinics, stress-management clinics, financial counseling, family counseling, and career counseling. Lowe's, for example, offers work/life seminars, smoking cessation clinics, and other assistance programs for its employees.[35] EAPs help reduce costs associated with poor productivity, absenteeism, and other workplace issues by helping employees deal with personal problems that contribute to these issues. For example, exercise and fitness programs reduce health insurance costs by helping employees stay healthy. Family counseling may help workers trying to cope with a divorce or other personal problems to better focus on their jobs.

Companies try to provide the benefits they believe their employees want, but diverse people may want different things. In recent years, some single workers have felt that co-workers with spouses and children seem to get "special breaks" and extra time off to deal with family issues. Some companies use flexible benefit programs to allow employees to choose the benefits they would like, up to a specified amount.

Entrepreneurship in Action

Urban Lending Solutions Hires Outside the Box

Urban Lending Solutions

Founders: Charles and Elisa Sanders

Founded: 2002, in Pittsburg, Pennsylvania

Success: Urban Lending Solutions generated revenue of $183.1 million in 2012.

In 2002, former professional athlete Charles Sanders and his wife, Elisa, founded Urban Lending Solutions (ULS), a real estate company in Pittsburg, Pennsylvania. The real estate industry is highly competitive and especially vulnerable to changes in the market. Because of this volatility in the market, Charles Sanders, who serves as CEO, takes a different approach to hiring employees. While other real estate companies focus on hiring seasoned professionals, Sanders looks for intellect and ambition in potential hires regardless of their experience. He has hired people ranging from managers at fast-food restaurants to the newly graduated. As a result, ULS has grown to more than 1,500 employees, a 257 percent increase since 2009.

ULS believes in the importance of employee training. It established its training program, called Urban University, to offer 15 courses meant to teach new hires everything they need to know, while preparing them to become adaptable when market conditions change. ULS's training and hiring approach has allowed the company to expand its services across the nation, retain valuable employees, and successfully respond to the difficulties of the latest housing market crash.[36]

Fringe benefits include sick leave, vacation pay, pension plans, health plans, and any other extra compensation. Soft benefits include perks that help balance life and work. They include onsite child care, spas, food service, and even laundry services and hair salons. These soft benefits motivate employees and give them more time to focus on their job.

Cafeteria benefit plans provide a financial amount to employees so that they can select the specific benefits that fit their needs. The key is making benefits flexible, rather than giving employees identical benefits. As firms go global, the need for cafeteria or flexible benefit plans becomes even more important. For some employees, benefits are a greater motivator and differentiator in jobs than wages. For many Starbucks employees who receive health insurance when working part time, this benefit could be the most important compensation.

Over the past two decades, the list of fringe benefits has grown dramatically, and new benefits are being added every year.

工会雇员管理
Managing Unionized Employees

LO 3-6

Employees who are dissatisfied with their working conditions or compensation have to negotiate with management to bring about change. Dealing with management on an individual basis is not always effective, however, so employees may organize themselves into **labor unions** to deal with employers and to achieve better pay, hours, and working conditions. Organized employees are backed by the power of a large group that can hire specialists to represent the entire union in its dealings with management. Union workers make significantly more than nonunion employees. The United States has a roughly 11.3 percent unionization rate. Figure 3.4 displays unionization rates by state. On average, the median usual weekly earnings of unionized full-time and salary workers are about $200 more than their non-union counterparts.[37]

工会
labor unions employee organizations formed to deal with employers for achieving better pay, hours, and working conditions

However, union growth has slowed in recent years, and prospects for growth do not look good. One reason is that most blue-collar workers, the traditional members

FIGURE 3.4 **Union Membership Rates by State**

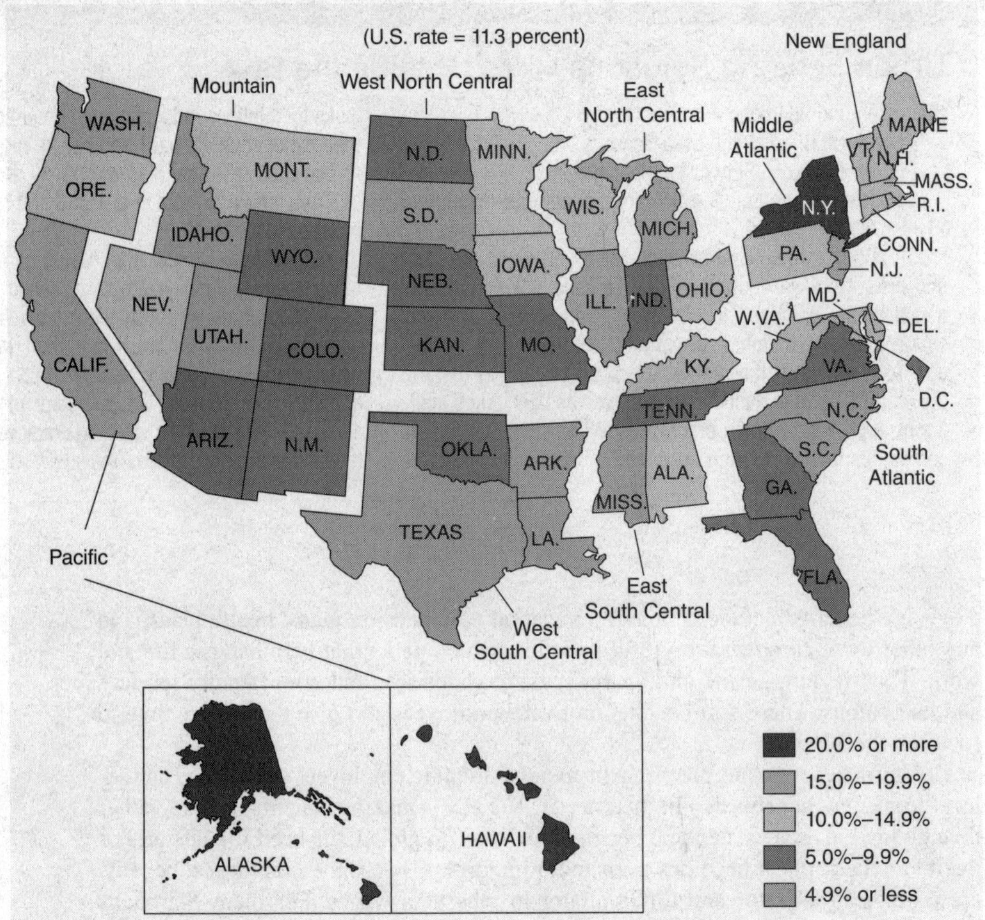

Source: Bureau of Labor Statistics, "Union Members—2013," January 24, 2014.

of unions, have already been organized. Factories have become more automated and need fewer blue-collar workers. The United States has shifted from a manufacturing to a service economy, further reducing the demand for blue-collar workers. Moreover, in response to foreign competition, U.S. companies are scrambling to find ways to become more productive and cost efficient. Job enrichment programs and participative management have blurred the line between management and workers. Because workers' say in the way plants are run is increasing, their need for union protection is decreasing.

Nonetheless, labor unions have been successful in organizing blue-collar manufacturing, government, and health care workers, as well as smaller percentages of employees in other industries. Consequently, significant aspects of HRM, particularly compensation, are dictated to a large degree by union contracts at many companies. Therefore, we'll take a brief look at collective bargaining and dispute resolution in this section.

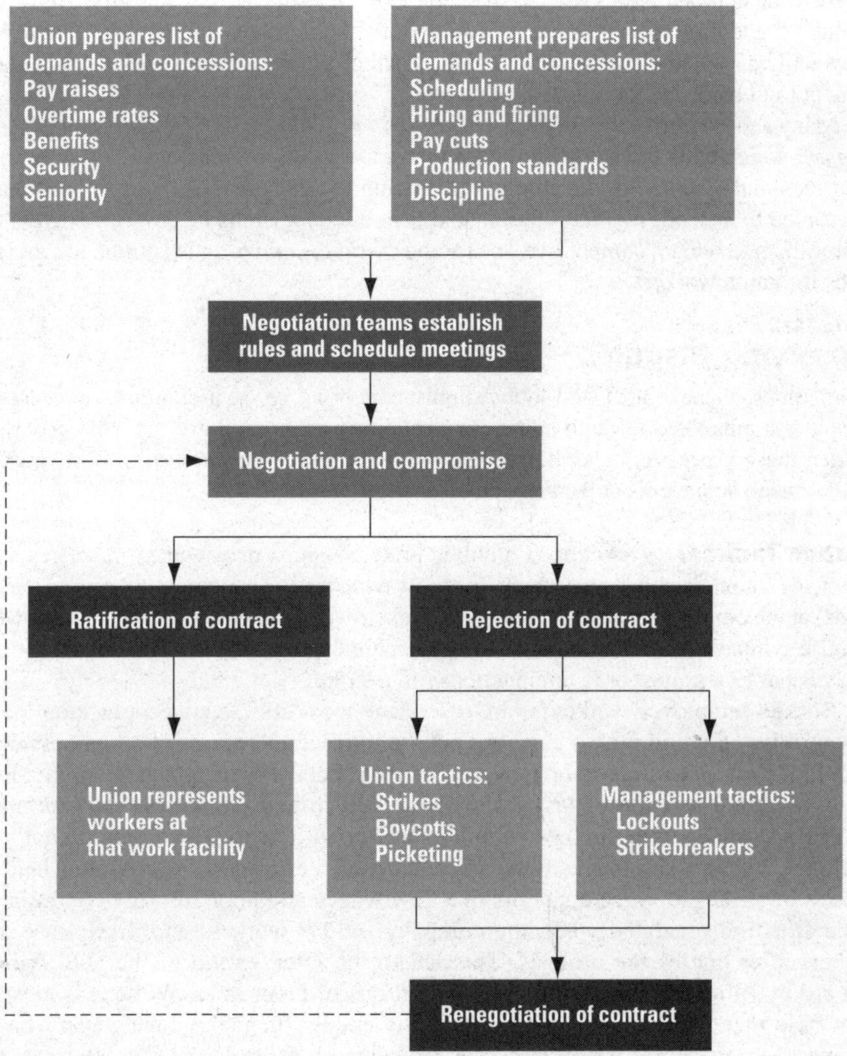

FIGURE 3.5
The Collective Bargaining Process

集体谈判
Collective Bargaining

Collective bargaining is the negotiation process through which management and unions reach an agreement about compensation, working hours, and working conditions for the bargaining unit (Figure 3.5). The objective of negotiations is to reach agreement about a **labor contract,** the formal, written document that spells out the relationship between the union and management for a specified period of time, usually two or three years.

In collective bargaining, each side tries to negotiate an agreement that meets its demands; compromise is frequently necessary. Management tries to negotiate a labor contract that permits the company to retain control over things like work schedules; the hiring and firing of workers; production standards; promotions, transfers, and separations; the span of management in each department; and discipline. Unions tend

集体谈判
collective bargaining
the negotiation process through which management and unions reach an agreement about compensation, working hours, and working conditions for the bargaining unit

劳动合同
labor contract
the formal, written document that spells out the relationship between the union and management for a specified period of time—usually two or three years

to focus on contract issues such as magnitude of wages; better pay rates for overtime, holidays, and undesirable shifts; scheduling of pay increases; and benefits. These issues will be spelled out in the labor contract, which union members will vote to either accept (and abide by) or reject.

Many labor contracts contain a *cost-of-living escalator* (or *adjustment*) *(COLA) clause,* which calls for automatic wage increases during periods of inflation to protect the "real" income of the employees. During tough economic times, unions may be forced to accept *givebacks*—wage and benefit concessions made to employers to allow them to remain competitive or, in some cases, to survive and continue to provide jobs for union workers.

解决纠纷
Resolving Disputes

Sometimes, management and labor simply cannot agree on a contract. Most labor disputes are handled through collective bargaining or through grievance procedures. When these processes break down, however, either side may resort to more drastic measures to achieve its objectives.

示威抗议
picketing
a public protest against management practices that involves union members marching and carrying antimanagement signs at the employer's plant or work site

罢工
strikes
employee walkouts; one of the most effective weapons of labor unions

联合抵制
boycott
an attempt to keep people from purchasing the products of a company

闭厂
lockout
management's version of a strike, wherein a work site is closed so that employees cannot go to work

劳动方策略

Labor Tactics. **Picketing** is a public protest against management practices and involves union members marching (often waving antimanagement signs and placards) at the employer's plant or work site. Picketing workers hope that their signs will arouse sympathy for their demands from the public and from other unions. Picketing may occur as a protest or in conjunction with a strike.

Strikes (employee walkouts) are one of the most effective weapons labor has. By striking, a union makes carrying out the normal operations of a business difficult at best and impossible at worst. Strikes receive widespread publicity, but they remain a weapon of last resort. However, in extreme cases, workers may organize a strike with the help of unions and coalitions to which they do not yet belong. Walmart employees, who are not unionized in the United States, held a series of strikes to voice concerns over low wages and poor working conditions. The situation escalated when the company fired 9 workers and disciplined 18 others after one of the protests. This led to the intervention of the U.S. Labor Board by filing a complaint alleging violations of labor laws. While it is mostly the case that the mere threat of a strike is enough to make management back down, there are times when the issues are heatedly debated and regulatory agencies become involved.[38]

A **boycott** is an attempt to keep people from purchasing the products of a company. In a boycott, union members are asked not to do business with the boycotted organization. Some unions may even impose fines on members who ignore the boycott. To gain further support for their objectives, a union involved in a boycott may also ask the public—through picketing and advertising—not to purchase the products of the picketed firm.

管理方策略

Management Tactics. Management's version of a strike is the **lockout;** management actually closes a work site so that employees cannot go to work. Lockouts are used, as a general rule, only when a union strike has partially shut down a plant and it seems less expensive for the plant to close completely. Kellogg locked out workers from its Memphis cereal plant for three months due to failure to reach a negotiating agreement on employees' wages and benefits. The situation escalated, with the company deciding to cut off the employees' health insurance for the duration of the strike.[39]

Strikebreakers, called "scabs" by striking union members, are people hired by management to replace striking employees. Managers hire strikebreakers to continue operations and reduce the losses associated with strikes—and to show the unions that they will not bow to their demands. Strikebreaking is generally a last-resort measure for management because it does great damage to the relationship between management and labor.

破坏罢工者
strikebreakers
people hired by management to replace striking employees; called "scabs" by striking union members

外部解决途径

Outside Resolution. Management and union members normally reach mutually agreeable decisions without outside assistance. Sometimes though, even after lengthy negotiations, strikes, lockouts, and other tactics, management and labor still cannot resolve a contract dispute. In such cases, they have three choices: conciliation, mediation, and arbitration. **Conciliation** brings in a neutral third party to keep labor and management talking. The conciliator has no formal power over union representatives or over management. The conciliator's goal is to get both parties to focus on the issues and to prevent negotiations from breaking down. Like conciliation, **mediation** involves bringing in a neutral third party, but the mediator's role is to suggest or propose a solution to the problem. The Association of Mineworkers and Construction Union (AMCU) and platinum workers had to meet with South African state mediators in order to resolve a $36 million per day dispute.[40] Mediators have no formal power over either labor or management. With **arbitration,** a neutral third party is brought in to settle the dispute, but the arbitrator's solution is legally binding and enforceable. Chevron won an arbitration case against the country of Ecuador regarding an ongoing 20-year dispute over pollution. The international arbitration panel ruled that the original case did not consider the fact that Ecuador had released the company from liability in the 1990s. Chevron was able to avoid a $19 billion penalty as a result.[41] Generally, arbitration takes place on a voluntary basis—management and labor must agree to it, and they usually split the cost (the arbitrator's fee and expenses) between them. Occasionally, management and labor submit to *compulsory arbitration,* in which an outside party (usually the federal government) requests arbitration as a means of eliminating a prolonged strike that threatens to disrupt the economy.

调解
conciliation
a method of outside resolution of labor and management differences in which a third party is brought in to keep the two sides talking

调停
mediation
a method of outside resolution of labor and management differences in which the third party's role is to suggest or propose a solution to the problem

仲裁
arbitration
settlement of a labor/management dispute by a third party whose solution is legally binding and enforceable

员工多元化的重要性
The Importance of Workforce Diversity

LO 3-7

Customers, employees, suppliers—all the participants in the world of business—come in different ages, genders, races, ethnicities, nationalities, and abilities, a truth that business has come to label **diversity.** Understanding this diversity means recognizing and accepting differences as well as valuing the unique perspectives such differences can bring to the workplace.

多元化
diversity
the participation of different ages, genders, races, ethnicities, nationalities, and abilities in the workplace

多元化的特征
The Characteristics of Diversity

When managers speak of diverse workforces, they typically mean differences in gender and race. While gender and race are important characteristics of diversity, others are also important. We can divide these differences into primary and secondary characteristics of diversity. In the lower segment of Figure 3.6, age, gender, race, ethnicity, abilities, and sexual orientation represent *primary characteristics* of diversity that are inborn and cannot be changed. In the upper section of Figure 3.6 are eight *secondary characteristics* of diversity—work background, income, marital status, military experience, religious beliefs, geographic location, parental status, and education—which *can* be changed. We acquire, change, and discard them as we progress through our lives.

connect

Need help understanding Mediation vs. Arbitration? Visit your Connect ebook video tab for a brief animated explanation.

FIGURE 3.6
Characteristics of Diversity

Source: Marilyn Loden and Judy B. Rosener, *Workforce America! Managing Employee Diversity as a Vital Resource*, 1991, p. 20. Used with permission. Copyright © 1991 The McGraw-Hill Companies.

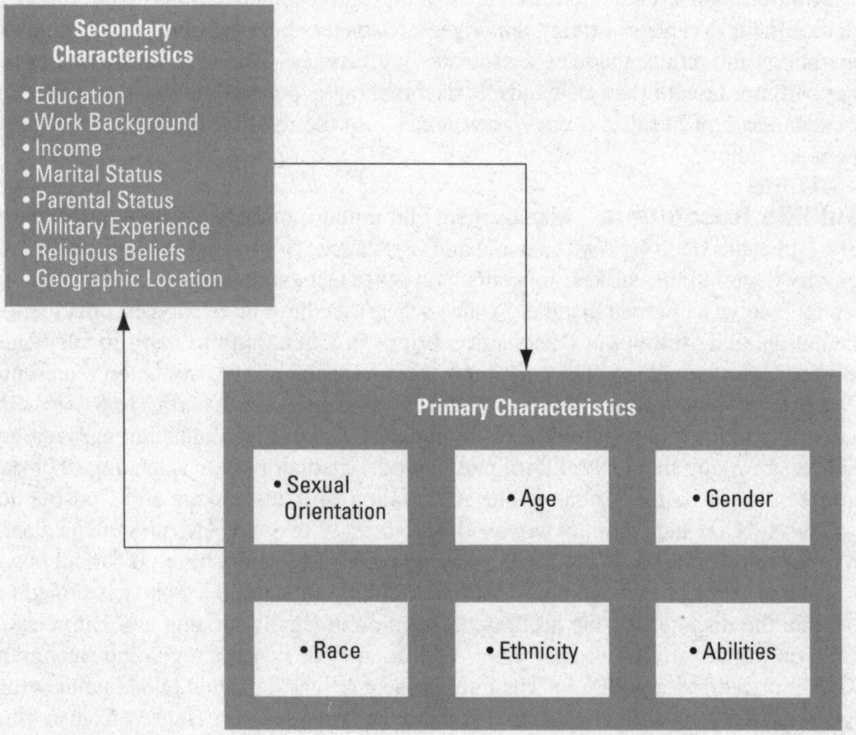

Defining characteristics of diversity as either primary or secondary enhances our understanding, but we must remember that each person is defined by the interrelation of all characteristics. In dealing with diversity in the workforce, managers must consider the complete person—not one or a few of a person's differences.

多元化为什么重要
Why Is Diversity Important?

Some of the major benefits of diversity include a wider range of employee perspectives, greater innovaiton and creativity, and the ability to target a diverse customer base more effectively.

The U.S. workforce is becoming increasingly diverse. Once dominated by white men, today's workforce includes significantly more women, African Americans, Hispanics, and other minorities, as well as disabled and older workers. The census bureau has predicted that by 2042, minorities will make up more than 50 percent of the U.S. population.[42] These groups have traditionally faced discrimination and higher unemployment rates and have been denied opportunities to assume leadership roles in corporate America. Consequently, more and more companies are trying to improve HRM programs to recruit, develop, and retain more diverse employees to better serve their diverse customers. Some firms are providing special programs such as sponsored affinity groups, mentoring programs, and special career development opportunities. Kaiser Permanente has incorporated diversity into its goals and corporate strategies. More than half of the company's board of directors consists of minorities, while 60 percent are women. This level of diversity has earned Kaiser Permanente fourth place on Diversity Inc.'s Top 50 Companies for Diversity list.[43] Diversity and equal rights is so important to Kaiser Permanente that it has established the Institute for Culturally Competent Care and the nine Centers of Excellence to pave the way for equal health care for all, including minorities, immigrants, and those with disabilities.[44] Table 3.9 shows the top companies for minorities according to a study by DiversityInc. Effectively managing diversity in the workforce involves cultivating and valuing its benefits and minimizing its problems.

TABLE 3.9
Top 50 Companies for Diversity

1. Novartis Pharmaceuticals Corporation	26. BASF
2. Sodexo	27. Eli Lilly and Company
3. Ernst & Young	28. Northrop Grumman
4. Kaiser Permanente	29. WellPoint
5. PricewaterhouseCoopers	30. Colgate-Palmolive
6. MasterCard Worldwide	31. Kellogg Company
7. Procter & Gamble	32. Dell
8. Prudential Financial	33. The Coca-Cola Company
9. Johnson & Johnson	34. The Walt Disney Company
10. AT&T	35. Kraft Foods Group
11. Deloitte	36. TIAA-CREF
12. Accenture	37. Allstate Insurance Company
13. Abbott	38. Toyota Motor North America
14. Merck & Co	39. Wyndham Worldwide
15. Cummins	40. Rockwell Collins
16. Marriott International	41. Medtronic
17. Wells Fargo	42. Time Warner
18. Cox Communications	43. Verizon Communications
19. Aetna	44. Comcast
20. General Mills	45. TD Bank
21. KPMG	46. Monsanto
22. Target	47. KeyCorp
23. IBM	48. JCPenney
24. ADP	49. AbbVie
25. New York Life	50. Nielsen

Source: "The 2014 DiversityInc Top 50 Companies for Diversity," DiversityInc, *2014.*

员工多元化的好处
The Benefits of Workforce Diversity

There are a number of benefits to fostering and valuing workforce diversity, including the following:

1. More productive use of a company's human resources.
2. Reduced conflict among employees of different ethnicities, races, religions, and sexual orientations as they learn to respect each other's differences.
3. More productive working relationships among diverse employees as they learn more about and accept each other.
4. Increased commitment to and sharing of organizational goals among diverse employees at all organizational levels.
5. Increased innovation and creativity as diverse employees bring new, unique perspectives to decision-making and problem-solving tasks.
6. Increased ability to serve the needs of an increasingly diverse customer base.[45]

Companies that do not value their diverse employees are likely to experience greater conflict, as well as prejudice and discrimination. Among individual employees, for example, racial slurs and gestures, sexist comments, and other behaviors by co-workers harm the individuals at whom such behavior is directed. The victims of such behavior may feel hurt, depressed, or even threatened and suffer from lowered self-esteem, all of which harm their productivity and morale. In such cases, women and minority employees may simply leave the firm, wasting the time, money, and other resources spent on hiring and training them. When discrimination comes from a supervisor, employees may also fear for their jobs. A discriminatory atmosphere not only can harm productivity and increase turnover, but it may also subject a firm to costly lawsuits and negative publicity.

Astute businesses recognize that they need to modify their human resources management programs to target the needs of *all* their diverse employees as well as the needs of the firm itself. They realize that the benefits of diversity are long term in nature and come only to those organizations willing to make the commitment. Most importantly, as workforce diversity becomes a valued organizational asset, companies spend less time managing conflict and more time accomplishing tasks and satisfying customers, which is, after all, the purpose of business.

平权行动
Affirmative Action

平权行动计划
affirmative action programs
legally mandated plans that try to increase job opportunities for minority groups by analyzing the current pool of workers, identifying areas where women and minorities are underrepresented, and establishing specific hiring and promotion goals, with target dates, for addressing the discrepancy

Many companies strive to improve their working environment through **affirmative action programs,** legally mandated plans that try to increase job opportunities for minority groups by analyzing the current pool of workers, identifying areas where women and minorities are underrepresented, and establishing specific hiring and promotion goals along with target dates for meeting those goals to resolve the discrepancy. Affirmative action began in 1965 as Lyndon B. Johnson issued the first of a series of presidential directives. It was designed to make up for past hiring and promotion prejudices, to overcome workplace discrimination, and to provide equal employment opportunities for blacks and whites. Since then, minorities have made solid gains.

Legislation passed in 1991 reinforces affirmative action but prohibits organizations from setting hiring quotas that might result in reverse discrimination. Reverse discrimination occurs when a company's policies force it to consider only minorities or women instead of concentrating on hiring the person who is best qualified. More companies are arguing that affirmative action stifles their ability to hire the best

Consider Ethics and Social Responsibility

Employee Privacy or Employer Vulnerability: The Role of Social Media in the Financial Industry

Since the advent of social media in the workplace, many states have begun passing legislation to prevent employers from monitoring their employees' social media activities. This is done to protect employee privacy. However, the Financial Industry Regulatory Authority and Wall Street are asking regulators to make an exception for employees in the financial industry. Worries of insider trading, potential Ponzi schemes, and influencing stock activity on the market are at the heart of this request. For instance, one CFO was fired after venting on social media using confidential financial information. Such information could negatively affect the firm if released early.

Regulators allow financial firms to communicate information through social media outlets as long as they disclose to the investor where, when, and how they plan to divulge this information. This could lead employees to believe it is also all right to discuss nonpublic information on social media. Financial firms are concerned that by protecting employee's privacy on social media, they become vulnerable to potential scandals involving the misappropriation of financial information, which could harm investors. While the requested amendment to the privacy laws will only be put to use if an employee is suspected of releasing unwarranted information, critics believe that such an exception will erode employee privacy altogether.[46]

Discussion Questions

1. What are advantages of laws forbidding employers from accessing employees' social media activities?
2. What are disadvantages of laws forbidding employers from accessing employees' social media activities?
3. Is there anything firms can do to keep employees from releasing nonpublic information over social media without infringing on their privacy?

employees, regardless of their minority status. Because of these problems, affirmative action became politically questionable.

员工管理的发展趋势
Trends in Management of the Workforce

As unemployment reached 10 percent during the last recession, businesses laid off almost 9 million employees. Even after the recession and financial crisis, many firms reduced hiring and pushed workers to spend more time on the job for the same or less pay. Because of the economic uncertainty, this post-recession austerity has pervaded the workplace and inflated U.S. productivity. While companies are squeezing workers to cut costs, they are also drawing clear lines between workers and managers and are reducing privileges and benefits.

Many employees are developing grievances, claiming that they are being overworked. The number of lawsuits filed by employees against their employers continues to rise. Many of the claims include working overtime without being appropriately compensated, being overworked to the point of physical injury, and not being compensated for time waiting for company mandated security checks.[47]

The nature of the workplace is changing as well. The increasing use of smart phones and tablet computers are blurring the lines between leisure and work time, with some employers calling employees after hours.[48] Employees themselves are mixing work and personal time by using social media in the office. In fact, theft of time is a major form of misconduct in the workplace. This is requiring companies to come up with new policies that limit how employees can use social media in the workplace. Clearly, technology is changing the dynamics of the workplace in both positive and negative ways.

It is important for human resources managers to be aware of legal issues regarding worker rights. Strict criteria—such as having management responsibilities, having advanced degrees, or making more than $455 a week—determine whether an employee is exempt from overtime pay.[49] Interestingly, although it might currently be legal for employers to request an applicant's Facebook password, employees who "rant" about their employers on Facebook can receive some form of legal protection. Under the National Labor Relations Act of 1935, certain private-sector employees are allowed to complain about working conditions and pay—which seems to apply to social media sites as well. Threats, on the other hand, are not protected.[50] Hence, human resources managers should understand these issues to ensure that an employee is not wrongfully terminated.

Despite the grim outlook of the past few years, hiring trends appear to be on the rise. Companies are finding that as consumer demands rise, their current employees are hitting the limits of productivity, requiring firms to hire more workers.[51] This will require firms to not only know about relevant employee laws, but also to understand how benefits and employee morale can contribute to overall productivity. Many of the most successful firms have discovered ways to balance costs with the well-being of their employees.

So You Want to Work in Human Resources

Managing human resources is a challenging and creative facet of a business. It is the department that handles the recruiting, hiring, training, and firing of employees. Because of the diligence and detail required in hiring and the sensitivity required in firing, human resources managers have a broad skill set. Human resources, therefore, is vital to the overall functioning of the business because without the right staff a firm will not be able to effectively carry out its plans. Like in basketball, a team is only as strong as its individual players, and those players must be able to work together and to enhance strengths and downplay weaknesses. In addition, a good human resources manager can anticipate upcoming needs and changes in the business, hiring in line with the dynamics of the market and organization.

Once a good workforce is in place, human resources managers must ensure that employees are properly trained and oriented and that they clearly understand some elements of what the organization expects. Hiring new people is expensive, time consuming, and turbulent; thus, it is imperative that all employees are carefully selected, trained, and motivated so that they will remain committed and loyal to the company. This is not an easy task, but it is one of the responsibilities of the human resources manager. Because even with references, a résumé, background checks, and an interview, it can be hard to tell how a person will fit in the organization—the HR manager needs to have skills to be able to anticipate how every individual will "fit in." Human resources jobs include compensation, labor relations, benefits, training, ethics, and compliance managers. All of the tasks associated with the interface with hiring, developing, and maintaining employee motivation come into play in human resources management. Jobs are diverse and salaries will depend on responsibilities, education, and experience.

One of the major considerations for an HR manager is workforce diversity. A multicultural, multiethnic workforce consisting of men and women will help to bring a variety of viewpoints and improve the quality and creativity of organizational decision making. Diversity is an asset and can help a company from having blindspots or harmony in thought, background, and perspective, which stifles good team decisions. However, a diverse workforce can present some management challenges. Human resources management is often responsible for managing diversity training and compliance to make sure employees do not violate the ethical culture of the organization or break the law. Different people have different goals, motivations, and ways of thinking about issues that are informed by their culture, religion, and the people closest to them. No one way of thinking is more right or more wrong than others, and they are all valuable. A human resources manager's job can become very complicated, however, because of diversity. To be good at human resources, you should be aware of the value of differences, strive to be culturally sensitive, and ideally should have a strong understanding and appreciation of different cultures and religions. Human resources managers' ability to manage diversity and those differences will affect their overall career success.

Review Your Understanding

Define human resources management, and explain its significance.

Human resources, or personnel, management refers to all the activities involved in determining an organization's human resources needs and acquiring, training, and compensating people to fill those needs. It is concerned with maximizing the satisfaction of employees and improving their efficiency to meet organizational objectives.

Summarize the processes of recruiting and selecting human resources for a company.

First, the human resources manager must determine the firm's future human resources needs and develop a strategy to meet them. Recruiting is the formation of a pool of qualified applicants from which management will select employees; it takes place both internally and externally. Selection is the process of collecting information about applicants and using that information to decide which ones to hire; it includes the application, interviewing, testing, and reference checking.

Discuss how workers are trained and their performance appraised.

Training teaches employees how to do their specific job tasks; development is training that augments the skills and knowledge of managers and professionals, as well as current employees. Appraising performance involves identifying an employee's strengths and weaknesses on the job. Performance appraisals may be subjective or objective.

Identify the types of turnover companies may experience, and explain why turnover is an important issue.

A promotion is an advancement to a higher-level job with increased authority, responsibility, and pay. A transfer is a move to another job within the company at essentially the same level and wage. Separations occur when employees resign, retire, are terminated, or are laid off. Turnovers due to separation are expensive because of the time, money, and effort required to select, train, and manage new employees.

Specify the various ways a worker may be compensated.

Wages are financial compensation based on the number of hours worked (time wages) or the number of units produced (piece wages). Commissions are a fixed amount or a percentage of a sale paid as compensation. Salaries are compensation calculated on a weekly, monthly, or annual basis, regardless of the number of hours worked or the number of items produced. Bonuses and profit sharing are types of financial incentives. Benefits are nonfinancial forms of compensation, such as vacation, insurance, and sick leave.

Discuss some of the issues associated with unionized employees, including collective bargaining and dispute resolution.

Collective bargaining is the negotiation process through which management and unions reach an agreement on a labor contract—the formal, written document that spells out the relationship written between the union and management. If labor and management cannot agree on a contract, labor union members may picket, strike, or boycott the firm, while management may lock out striking employees, hire strikebreakers, or form employers' associations. In a deadlock, labor disputes may be resolved by a third party—a conciliator, mediator, or arbitrator.

Describe the importance of diversity in the workforce.

When companies value and effectively manage their diverse workforces, they experience more productive use of human resources, reduced conflict, better work relationships among workers, increased commitment to and sharing of organizational goals, increased innovation and creativity, and enhanced ability to serve diverse customers.

Assess an organization's efforts to reduce its workforce size and manage the resulting effects.

Based on the material in this chapter, you should be able to answer the questions posed in "Solve the Dilemma" on page 319 and evaluate the company's efforts to manage the human consequences of its downsizing.

Revisit the World of Business

1. Describe Cirque du Soleil's recruitment and interview process.
2. Why is creativity of new hires important to Cirque du Soleil?
3. What are some of the difficulties in hiring such a diverse group of performers?

Learn the Terms

affirmative action programs
arbitration
benefits
bonuses
boycott
collective bargaining
commission
conciliation
development
diversity
human resources management (HRM)
job analysis
job description
job specification
labor contract
labor unions
lockout
mediation
orientation
picketing
profit sharing
promotion
recruiting
salary
selection
separations
strikebreakers
strikes
Title VII of the Civil Rights Act
training
transfer
turnover
wage/salary survey
wages

Check Your Progress

1. Distinguish among job analysis, job descriptions, and job specifications. How do they relate to planning in human resources management?
2. What activities are involved in acquiring and maintaining the appropriate level of qualified human resources? Name the stages of the selection process.
3. What are the two types of training programs? Relate training to kinds of jobs.
4. What is the significance of performance appraisal? How do managers appraise employees?
5. Why does turnover occur? List the types of turnover. Why do businesses want to reduce turnover due to separations?
6. Relate wages, salaries, bonuses, and benefits to Herzberg's distinction between hygiene and motivation factors. How does the form of compensation relate to the type of job?
7. What is the role of benefits? Name some examples of benefits.
8. Describe the negotiation process through which management and unions reach an agreement on a contract.
9. Besides collective bargaining and the grievance procedures, what other alternatives are available to labor and management to handle labor disputes?
10. What are the benefits associated with a diverse workforce?

Get Involved

1. Although many companies screen applicants and test employees for illegal drug use, such testing is somewhat controversial. Find some companies in your community that test applicants and/or employees for drugs. Why do they have such a policy? How do the employees feel about it? Using this information, debate the pros and cons of drug testing in the workplace.
2. If collective bargaining and the grievance procedures have not been able to settle a current labor dispute, what tactics would you and other employees adopt? Which tactics would be best for which situations? Give examples.
3. Find some examples of companies that value their diverse workforces, perhaps some of the companies mentioned in the chapter. In what ways have these firms derived benefits from promoting cultural diversity? How have they dealt with the problems associated with cultural diversity?

Build Your Skills

Appreciating and Valuing Diversity

Background

Here's a quick self-assessment to get you to think about diversity issues and evaluate the behaviors you exhibit that reflect your level of appreciation of other cultures:

Do you . . .	Regularly	Sometimes	Never
1. Make a conscious effort not to think stereotypically?			
2. Listen with interest to the ideas of people who don't think like you do?			
3. Respect other people's opinions, even when you disagree?			
4. Spend time with friends who are not your age, race, gender, or the same economic status and education?			

continued

Do you . . .	Regularly	Sometimes	Never
5. Believe your way is *not* the only way?			
6. Adapt well to change and new situations?			
7. Enjoy traveling, seeing new places, eating different foods, and experiencing other cultures?			
8. Try not to offend or hurt others?			
9. Allow extra time to communicate with someone whose first language is not yours?			
10. Consider the effect of cultural differences on the messages you send and adjust them accordingly?			

Scoring

Number of **Regularly** checks _____ multiplied by 5 = _____
Number of **Sometimes** checks _____ multiplied by 3 = _____
Number of **Never** checks _____ multiplied by 0 = _____
TOTAL _____

Indications from score

40–50 You appear to understand the importance of valuing diversity and exhibit behaviors that support your appreciation of diversity.

6–39 You appear to have a basic understanding of the importance of valuing diversity and exhibit some behaviors that support that understanding.

13–5 You appear to lack a thorough understanding of the importance of valuing diversity and exhibit only some behaviors related to valuing diversity.

0–1 You appear to lack an understanding of valuing diversity and exhibit few, if any, behaviors of an individual who appreciates and values diversity.

Task

In a small group or class discussion, share the results of your assessment. After reading the following list of ways you can increase your knowledge and understanding of other cultures, select one of the items that you have done and share how it helped you learn more about another culture. Finish your discussion by generating your own ideas on other ways you can learn about and understand other cultures and fill in those ideas on the blank lines on page 319.

- Be alert to and take advantage of opportunities to talk to and get to know people from other races and ethnic groups. You can find them in your neighborhood, in your classes, at your fitness center, at a concert or sporting event—just about anywhere you go. Take the initiative to strike up a conversation and show a genuine interest in getting to know the other person.
- Select a culture you're interested in and immerse yourself in that culture. Read novels, look at art, take courses, see plays.
- College students often have unique opportunities to travel inexpensively to other countries—for example, as a member of a performing arts group, with a humanitarian mission group, or as part of a college course studying abroad. Actively seek out travel opportunities that will expose you to as many cultures as possible during your college education.
- Study a foreign language.

- Expand your taste buds. The next time you're going to go to a restaurant, instead of choosing that old familiar favorite, find a restaurant that serves ethnic food you've never tried before.
- Many large metropolitan cities sponsor ethnic festivals, particularly in the summertime, where you can go and take in the sights and sounds of other cultures. Take advantage of these opportunities to have a fun time learning about cultures that are different from yours.
- ______________________________
- ______________________________

Solve the Dilemma LO 3-8

Morale among the Survivors

Medallion Corporation manufactures quality carpeting and linoleum for homes throughout the United States. A recession and subsequent downturn in home sales has sharply cut the company's sales. Medallion found itself in the unenviable position of having to lay off hundreds of employees in the home office (the manufacturing facilities) as well as many salespeople. Employees were called in on Friday afternoon and told about their status in individual meetings with their supervisors. The laid-off employees were given one additional month of work and a month of severance pay, along with the opportunity to sign up for classes to help with the transition, including job search tactics and résumé writing.

Several months after the cutbacks, morale was at an all-time low for the company, although productivity had improved. Medallion brought in consultants, who suggested that the leaner, flatter organizational structure would be suitable for more team activities. Medallion therefore set up task forces and teams to deal with employee concerns, but the diversity of the workforce led to conflict and misunderstandings among team members. Medallion is evaluating how to proceed with this new team approach.

Discussion Questions

1. What did Medallion's HRM department do right in dealing with the employees who were laid off?
2. What are some of the potential problems that must be dealt with after an organization experiences a major trauma such as massive layoffs?
3. What can Medallion do to make the team approach work more smoothly? What role do you think diversity training should play?

Build Your Business Plan

Managing Human Resources

Now is the time to start thinking about the employees you will need to hire to implement your business plan. What kinds of background/skills are you going to look for in potential employees? Are you going to require a certain amount of work experience?

When you are starting a business, you are often only able to hire part-time employees because you cannot afford to pay the benefits for a full-time employee. Remember at the end of the last chapter we discussed how important it is to think of ways to motivate your employees when you cannot afford to pay them what you would like.

You need to consider how you are going to recruit your employees. When you are first starting your business, it is often a good idea to ask people you respect (and not necessarily members of your family) for any recommendations of potential employees they might have. You probably won't be able to afford to advertise in the classifieds, so announcements in sources such as church bulletins or community bulletin boards should be considered as an excellent way to attract potential candidates with little, if any, investment.

Finally, you need to think about hiring employees from diverse backgrounds, especially if you are considering targeting diverse segments. The more diverse your employees, the greater the chance you will be able to draw in diverse customers.

See for Yourself Videocase

The Importance of Hollywood Labor Unions

You might be familiar with unions for teachers or autoworkers. But what about unions for actors, radio artists, and screenwriters? Because we tend to view Hollywood as a glamorous place, we are tempted to view unions as unnecessary for these types of professions. Yet Hollywood unions were, and continue to be, important players in the careers of Hollywood artists.

When actors first became mainstream in the early 20th century, working conditions for the industry included long work weeks and low pay. Studios essentially "owned" their artists, which meant that rival studios would not hire actors or actresses once their contracts ended. Actors were forced to work for the same studio to advance their careers. Negotiations with studios often proved fruitless.

Because strikes can be so disruptive and risky, they are often used as a last resort. Yet, in 1919 the Actors' Equity Association, a union for theatrical performers, and the American Federation of Labor staged a Broadway strike to protest harsh working conditions. The strike resulted in a five-year contract and promises to improve labor conditions. Although the event happened off Broadway and not in Hollywood, it would inspire other artists to begin forming their own unions.

Working conditions might have improved somewhat for theatrical actors, but radio artists, film actors, and screenwriters still had to bear with hard conditions. For instance, radio artists might do an entire show and then receive only a dollar. Film actors would work around the clock with few (if any) breaks. Screenwriters experienced salary cuts. As individuals, these artists did not have much bargaining power with studios. Realizing that banding together could improve conditions, the Masquers Club (later the Screen Actors Guild of America) was created in 1925. It was followed by the Screenwriters Guild (later renamed the Writers Guild of America) in 1933 and the American Federation of Radio Artists in 1937.

It would take lawsuits, strikes, and hardline negotiations for Hollywood artists to receive more rights. This often required artists to take risks such as suspensions or firings in the hope of better treatment. In 1988, the Writers Guild of America organized the longest strike in Hollywood history after disagreements with producers over payments and creative rights. The strike, which lasted five months, was estimated to cost the industry $500 million.

Now that working conditions seem to have improved, it might be tempting to discard Hollywood unions as no longer useful. Yet, even today, conflicts often occur between artists and studios. For instance, the Screen Actors Guild of America (SAG) watches to make sure that low-budget actors know their rights and are not exploited by producers. Unequal treatment still happens in the entertainment industry. For instance, minorities and female actors/actresses still tend to be paid less than Caucasian and male actors. The introduction of new media venues, particularly the Internet, may also warrant additional negotiations.

To address these challenges, many unions are banding together to address mutual concerns in the industry. In 2012, SAG united with the American Federation of Television and Radio Artists (AFTRA). This increases the bargaining power of the combined union. Additionally, Hollywood unions work closely with the American Federation of Labor and Congress of Industrial Organizations (AFL-CIO), which represents a federation of labor unions. The merger between SAG and AFTRA creates solidarity in the industry's unions through the formation of an Industry Coordinating Committee. This allows for coordination of activity among 10 or 12 major unions within the industry.

Although these unions are for movie stars and other artists, the goal is much the same as for other unions across the nation. As the industry expands, Hollywood unions feel that they must work together to secure benefits for their members while striving to arrive at mutually beneficial agreements with studios, producers, and other stakeholders in the entertainment industry.[52]

Discussion Questions

1. Why are Hollywood labor unions considered necessary?
2. Why is striking often avoided if possible?
3. Why do you think unions in the entertainment industry are banding together?

You can find the related video in the Video Library in Connect. Ask your instructor how you can access Connect.

Team Exercise

Form groups and go to monster.com and look up job descriptions for positions in business (account executive in advertising, marketing manager, human resource director, production supervisor, financial analyst, bank teller, etc.). What are the key requirements for the position that you have been assigned (education, work experience, language/computer skills, etc.)? Does the position announcement provide a thorough understanding of the job? Was any key information that you would have expected omitted? Report your findings to the class.

Appendix 附录

Personal Career Plan 个人职业规划

The tools and techniques used in creating a business plan are just as useful in designing a plan to help sell yourself to potential employers. The outline in this appendix is designed to assist you in writing a personalized plan that will help you achieve your career goals. While this outline follows the same general format found in Appendix A, it has been adapted to be more relevant to career planning. Answering the questions presented in this outline will enable you to:

1. Organize and structure the data and information you collect about job prospects, the overall job market, and your competition.
2. Use this information to better understand your own personal strengths and weaknesses, as well as recognize the opportunities and threats that exist in your career development.
3. Develop goals and objectives that will capitalize on your strengths.
4. Develop a personalized strategy that will give you a competitive advantage.
5. Outline a plan for implementing your personalized strategy.

As you work through the following outline, it is very important that you be honest with yourself. If you do not possess a strength in a given area, it is important to recognize that fact. Similarly, do not overlook your weaknesses. The viability of your SWOT analysis and your strategy depend on how well you have identified all of the relevant issues in an honest manner.

I. Summary

If you choose to write a summary, do so after you have written the entire plan. It should provide a brief overview of the strategy for your career. State your career objectives and what means you will use to achieve those objectives.

II. Situation Analysis

A. The External Environment

1. Competition

a. Who are your major competitors? What are their characteristics (number and growth in the number of graduates, skills, target employers)? Competitors to consider include peers at the same college or in the same degree field, peers at different colleges or in different degree fields, and graduates of trade, technical, or community colleges.

b. What are the key strengths and weaknesses of the total pool of potential employees (or recent college graduates)?

c. What are other college graduates doing in terms of developing skills, networking, showing a willingness to relocate, and promoting themselves to potential employers?

d. What are the current trends in terms of work experience versus getting an advanced degree?

e. Is your competitive set likely to change in the future? If so, how? Who are these new competitors likely to be?

2. Economic conditions

a. What are the general economic conditions of the country, region, state, and local area in which you live or in which you want to relocate?

b. Overall, are potential employers optimistic or pessimistic about the economy?

c. What is the overall outlook for major job/career categories? Where do potential employers seem to be placing their recruitment and hiring emphasis?

d. What is the trend in terms of starting salaries for major job/career categories?

3. Political trends

a. Have recent elections changed the political landscape so that certain industries or companies are now more or less attractive as potential employers?

4. Legal and regulatory factors

a. What changes in international, federal, state, or local laws and regulations are being proposed that would affect your job/career prospects?

b. Have recent court decisions made it easier or harder for you to find employment?

c. Have global trade agreements changed in any way that makes certain industries or companies more or less attractive as potential employers?

5. Changes in technology

a. What impact has changing technology had on potential employers in terms of their need for employees?

b. What technological changes will affect the way you will have to work and compete for employment in the future?

c. What technological changes will affect the way you market your skills and abilities to potential employers?

d. How do technological advances threaten to make your skills and abilities obsolete?

6. Cultural trends

a. How are society's demographics and values changing? What effect will these changes have on your:

(1) Skills and abilities:
(2) Career/lifestyle choices:
(3) Ability to market yourself:
(4) Willingness to relocate:
(5) Required minimum salary:

b. What problems or opportunities are being created by changes in the cultural diversity of the labor pool and the requirements of potential employers?

c. What is the general attitude of society regarding the particular skills, abilities, and talents that you possess and the career/lifestyle choices that you have made?

B. The Employer Environment

1. Who are your potential employers?

a. Identify characteristics: industry, products, size, growth, profitability, hiring practices, union/nonunion, employee needs, etc.

b. Geographic characteristics: home office, local offices, global sites, expansion, etc.

c. Organizational culture: mission statement, values, priorities, employee training, etc.

d. In each organization, who is responsible for recruiting and selecting new employees?

2. What do your potential employers look for in new employees?

a. What are the basic or specific skills and abilities that employers are looking for in new employees?

b. What are the basic or specific needs that are fulfilled by the skills and abilities that you *currently* possess and that other potential employees currently possess?

c. How well do your skills and abilities (and those of your competitors) currently meet the needs of potential employers?

d. How are the needs of potential employers expected to change in the future?

3. What are the recent hiring practices of your potential employers?

a. How many employees are being hired? What combination of skills and abilities do these new hires possess?

b. Is the growth or decline in hiring related to the recent expansion or downsizing of markets and/or territories? Changes in technology?

c. Are there major hiring differences between large and small companies? If so, why?

4. Where and how do your potential employers recruit new employees?

- **a.** Where do employers make contact with potential employees?
  - (1) College placement offices:
  - (2) Job/career fairs:
  - (3) Internship programs:
  - (4) Headhunting firms:
  - (5) Unsolicited applications:
  - (6) The Internet:
- **b.** Do potential employers place a premium on experience or are they willing to hire new graduates without experience?

5. When do your potential employers recruit new employees?

- **a.** Does recruiting follow a seasonal pattern or do employers recruit new employees on an ongoing basis?

C. Personal Assessment

1. Review of personal goals, objectives, and performance

- **a.** What are your personal goals and objectives in terms of employment, career, lifestyle, geographic preferences, etc.?
- **b.** Are your personal goals and objectives consistent with the realities of the labor market? Why or why not?
- **c.** Are your personal goals and objectives consistent with recent changes in the external or employer environments? Why or why not?
- **d.** How are your current strategies for success working in areas such as course performance, internships, networking, job leads, career development, interviewing skills, etc.?
- **e.** How does your current performance compare to that of your peers (competitors)? Are they performing well in terms of course performance, internships, networking, job leads, career development, interviewing skills, etc.?
- **f.** If your performance is improving, what actions can you take to ensure that your performance continues in this direction?

2. Inventory of personal skills and resources

- **a.** What do you consider to be your marketable skills? This list should be as comprehensive as possible and include areas such as interpersonal skills, organizational skills, technological skills, communication skills (oral and written), networking/teambuilding skills, etc.
- **b.** Considering the current and future needs of your potential employers, what important skills are you lacking?
- **c.** Other than personal skills, what do you consider to be your other career-enhancing resources? This list should be as comprehensive as possible and include areas such as financial resources (to pay for additional training, if necessary), personal contacts or "connections" with individuals who can assist your career development, specific degrees or certificates you hold, and intangible resources (family name, prestige of your educational institution, etc.).
- **d.** Considering the current and future needs of your potential employers, what important resources are you lacking?

III. SWOT Analysis (your personal strengths and weaknesses and the opportunities and threats that may impact your career)

A. Personal Strengths

1. Three key strengths
   - **a.** Strength 1:
   - **b.** Strength 2:
   - **c.** Strength 3:
2. How do these strengths allow you to meet the needs of your potential employers?
3. How do these strengths compare to those of your peers/competitors? Do these strengths give you an advantage relative to your peers/competitors?

B. Personal Weaknesses

1. Three key weaknesses
   a. Weakness 1:
   b. Weakness 2:
   c. Weakness 3:
2. How do these weaknesses cause you to fall short of meeting the needs of your potential employers?
3. How do these weaknesses compare to those of your peers/competitors? Do these weaknesses put you at a disadvantage relative to your peers/competitors?

C. Career Opportunities

1. Three key career opportunities
   a. Opportunity 1:
   b. Opportunity 2:
   c. Opportunity 3:
2. How are these opportunities related to serving the needs of your potential employers?
3. What actions must be taken to capitalize on these opportunities in the short term? In the long term?

D. Career Threats

1. Three key career threats
   a. Threat 1:
   b. Threat 2:
   c. Threat 3:
2. How are these threats related to serving the needs of your potential employers?
3. What actions must be taken to prevent these threats from limiting your capabilities in the short term? In the long term?

E. The SWOT Matrix

F. Matching, Converting, Minimizing, and Avoiding Strategies

1. How can you match your strengths to your opportunities to better serve the needs of your potential employers?
2. How can you convert your weaknesses into strengths?
3. How can you convert your threats into opportunities?
4. How can you minimize or avoid those weaknesses and threats that cannot be converted successfully?

IV. Resources

A. Financial

1. Do you have the financial resources necessary to undertake and successfully complete this plan (that is, preparation/duplication/mailing of a résumé; interviewing costs, including proper attire; etc.)?

B. Human

1. Is the industry in which you are interested currently hiring? Are companies in your area currently hiring?

C. Experience and Expertise

1. Do you have experience from either part-time or summer employment that could prove useful in your current plan?
2. Do you have the required expertise or skills to qualify for a job in your desired field? If not, do you have the resources to obtain them?

V. Strategies

A. Objective(s)

1. Potential employer A:
   a. Descriptive characteristics:
   b. Geographic locations:
   c. Culture/values/mission:
   d. Basic employee needs:
   e. Recruiting/hiring practices:
   f. Employee training/compensation practices:
   g. Justification for selection:
2. Potential employer B:
   a. Descriptive characteristics:
   b. Geographic locations:
   c. Culture/values/mission:
   d. Basic employee needs:
   e. Recruiting/hiring practices:
   f. Employee training/compensation practices:
   g. Justification for selection:

B. Strategy(ies) for Using Capabilities and Resources

1. Strategy A (to meet the needs of potential employer A)
   a. Personal skills, abilities, and resources
      (1) Description of your skills and abilities:

(2) Specific employer needs that your skills/abilities can fulfill:
(3) Differentiation relative to peers/competitors (why should *you* be hired?):
(4) Additional resources that you have to offer:
(5) Needed or expected starting salary:
(6) Expected employee benefits:
(7) Additional employer-paid training that you require:
(8) Willingness to relocate:
(9) Geographic areas to target:
(10) Corporate divisions or offices to target:
(11) Summary of overall strategy:
(12) Tactics for standing out among the crowd of potential employees:
(13) Point of contact with potential employer:
(14) Specific elements
(a) Résumé:
(b) Internships:
(c) Placement offices:
(d) Job fairs:
(e) Personal contacts:
(f) Unsolicited:
(15) Specific objectives and budget:

2. Strategy B (to meet the needs of potential employer B)

a. Personal skills, abilities, and resources
(1) Description of your skills and abilities:
(2) Specific employer needs that your skills/abilities can fulfill:
(3) Differentiation relative to peers/competitors (why should *you* be hired?):
(4) Additional resources that you have to offer:
(5) Needed or expected starting salary:
(6) Expected employee benefits:
(7) Additional employer-paid training that you require:
(8) Willingness to relocate:
(9) Geographic areas to target:
(10) Corporate divisions or offices to target:
(11) Summary of overall strategy:
(12) Tactics for standing out among the crowd of potential employees:
(13) Point of contact with potential employer:
(14) Specific elements
(a) Résumé:
(b) Internships:
(c) Placement offices:
(d) Job fairs:
(e) Personal contacts:
(f) Unsolicited:
(15) Specific objectives and budget:

C. Strategy Summary

1. How does strategy A (B) give you a competitive advantage in serving the needs of potential employer A (B)?

2. Is this competitive advantage sustainable? Why or why not?

VI. Financial Projections and Budgets

A. Do you have a clear idea of your budgetary requirements (for example, housing, furnishings, clothing, transportation, food, other living expenses)?

B. Will the expected salaries/benefits from potential employers meet these requirements? If not, do you have an alternative plan (that is, a different job choice, a second job, requesting a higher salary)?

VII. Controls and Evaluation

A. Performance Standards

1. What do you have to offer?
Corrective actions that can be taken if your skills, abilities, and resources do not match the needs of potential employers:

2. Are you worth it?
Corrective actions that can be taken if potential employers do not think your skills/abilities are worth your asking price:

3. Where do you want to go?
Corrective actions that can be taken if potential employers do not offer you

a position in a preferred geographic location:

4. How will you stand out among the crowd?
Corrective actions that can be taken if your message is not being heard by potential employers or is not reaching the right people:

B. Monitoring Procedures

1. What types and levels of formal control mechanisms are in place to ensure the proper implementation of your plan?
   a. Are your potential employers hiring?
   b. Do you need additional training/education?
   c. Have you allocated sufficient time to your career development?
   d. Are your investments in career development adequate?
      (1) Training/education:
      (2) Networking/making contacts:
      (3) Wardrobe/clothing:
      (4) Development of interviewing skills:
   e. Have you done your homework on potential employers?
   f. Have you been involved in an internship program?
   g. Have you attended job/career fairs?
   h. Are you using the resources of your placement center?
   i. Are you committed to your career development?

C. Performance Analysis

1. Number/quality/potential of all job contacts made:
2. Number of job/career fairs attended and quality of the job leads generated:
3. Number of résumés distributed:
   a. Number of potential employers who responded:
   b. Number of negative responses:
4. Number of personal interviews:
5. Number/quality of job offers:

Notes 注释

Chapter 1

1. David A. Kaplan, "Inside Mars," *Fortune*, 73–82; "Mars," *Forbes*; "100 Best Companies to Work For: Mars," *CNN Money*, 2013; "Brands," Mars website.
2. Dan Heath and Chip Heath, "Business Advice from Van Halen," *Fast Company*, March 1, 2010.
3. Google, "Benefits".
4. "How Much Does Absenteeism Cost Your Business," The Perfect Labor Storm 2.0, December 10, 2008.
5. Brad Stone, "Costco CEO Craig Jelinek Leads the Cheapest, Happiest Company in the World," *Bloomberg Businessweek*, June 6, 2013.
6. Equilar Inc., "20 Top Paid CEOs," *CNN Money*, April 8, 2013.
7. Jillian Berman, "Wegmans Improves Its Bottom Line by Helping Employees Shrink Their Waistlines," *The Huffington Post*, August 5, 2013; "100 Best Companies to Work For: Wegmans Food Markets," *CNN Money*, 2014; Ariel Schwartz, "Greenpeace Ranks Sustainable Seafood in Grocery Stores, Wegmans Tops List," *Fast Company*, June 30, 2009; David Rohde, "The Anti-Walmart: The Secret Sauce of Wegmans Is People," *The Atlantic*, March 23, 2012; John Failla, "An Inside Look at Wegmans' Sustainability Efforts," *Green Retail Decisions*, April 14, 2011.
8. Fortune, "100 Best Companies to Work For—USAA," *CNN Money*, 2014; Fortune, "100 Best Companies to Work For—Genentech," *CNN Money*, 2014.
9. "25 Well-Paying Jobs That Most People Overlook (and Why)," *Business Pundit*.
10. Christina Couch, "10 Companies with Excellent Customer Service," *The Huffington Post*, August 15, 2013.
11. Douglas McGregor, *The Human Side of Enterprise* (New York: McGraw-Hill, 1960), pp. 33–34.
12. Hadley Malcolm, "CEO Close Up: Jay Stein's Personal Stein Mart Touch," *USA Today*, October 23, 2013; Press Release, "Stein Mart Launches Online Store," *The Wall Street Journal*, September 6, 2013; Stein Mart, "About Us," Stein Mart website; "Stein Mart Inc (SMRT:NASDAQ GS)," *Bloomberg Businessweek*.
13. Douglas McGregor, *The Human Side of Enterprise* (New York: McGraw-Hill, 1960), pp. 33–34.
14. Richard Branson, "Richard Branson on Giving Your Employees Freedom," *Entrepreneur*, December 31, 2012.
15. Jon L. Pierce, Tatiana Kostova, and Kurt T. Kirks, "Toward a Theory of Psychological Ownership in Organizations, *Academy of Management Review*, 26, no. 2 (2001), p. 298.
16. Liz Rappaport, "Goldman Cuts Blankfein's Bonus," *The Wall Street Journal*, February 4, 2012.
17. Ethics Resource Center, *2011 National Business Ethics Survey: Ethics in Transition* (Arlington, VA: Ethics Resource Center, 2012), p. 16.
18. Archie Carroll, "Carroll: Do We Live in a Cheating Culture?" *Athens Banner-Herald*, February 21, 2004.
19. Geoff Colvin, "How Top Companies Breed Stars," September 20, 2007.
20. Donald Liebenson, "Home Is Where the Work Is (Mostly for Men)," *Millionaire Corner*, March 5, 2014.
21. Robert Preidt, "Workplace Flexibility Can Boost Healthy Behaviors," *ABC News*, March 23, 2008.
22. My Guides USA.com, "Which Jobs Offer Flexible Work Schedules?" .
23. Randy Mayers, "The Great Debate: Should You Let Employees Work from Home?" *Entrepreneur*, June 3, 2013; Rick Hampson, "Boss vs. You," USA Today, March 12, 2013, pp. 1A–2A; Anita Bruzzese, "On the Job: Act Like an Entrepreneur Even If You're Not," *USA Today*, June 30, 2012.
24. Global Workplace Analytics, "Latest Telecommuting Statistics".
25. PGi, "Telecommuting Reduces Stress and Increases Productivity According to PGi Survey," *PR Newswire*, March 3, 2014; PR Web, "Fortune 500 Companies Are Looking for People to Work Remotely (Work From Home)," January 26, 2014.
26. Dori Meinert, "Make Telecommuting Pay Off," *Society for Human Resource Management*, June 1, 2011.
27. "Best Places For Business and Careers," *Forbes*, March 25, 2009.
28. "Best Places for Businesses and Careers 2013," *Forbes*, 2014.
29. "100 Best Companies to Work for 2009," *Fortune*; "The Container Store: An Employee-Centric Retailer," UNM Daniels Fund Business Ethics Initiative; Fortune 100 Best Companies to Work For, "The Container Store," *CNN Money*, 2013; The Container Store, "Employee-First Culture"; Bureau of Labor Statistics, "How to Become a Retail Sales Worker," January 8, 2014; The Container Store, "Communication IS Leadership"; The Container Store, "Happy National We Love Our Employees Day," February 13, 2014; The Container Store, "Great Benefits"; Maria Halkias, "The Container Store Set Up an Emergency Fund for Its Employee," *Dallas News*, February 14, 2014.

Chapter 2

1. Erika Fry, "How CarMax Cares," *Fortune*, April 8, 2013, p. 21; CarMax website, "CarMax Culture and Values"; Michael Myser, "The Wal-Mart of Used Cars," *CNN Money*, October 2, 2006.
2. Horace Dediu, "Understanding Apple's Organizational Structure," *Asymco*, July 3, 2013; Sam Grobart,

"How Samsung Became the World's No. 1 Smartphone Maker," *Bloomberg Businessweek*, March 28, 2013; Jay Yarow, "Apple's New Organizational Structure Could Help It Move Faster," *Business Insider*, May 1, 2013.

3. Reed Hastings, "How to Set Your Employees Free: Reed Hastings," *Bloomberg Businessweek*, April 12, 2012; Dan Lyons, "Advice on Corporate Culture From Netflix's Former Chief Talent Officer," *HubSpot*, May 7, 2013.
4. "A New Future for Toms Shoes, Tweed Shire and Room to Read," *Reputation Report*, August 7, 2009; "Our Movement," TOMS Shoes.
5. "Best Companies to Work For: Happy Campers," *CNNMoney*; Christopher Palmeri, "Zappos Retails Its Culture," *Bloomberg Businessweek*, December 30, 2009.
6. Rachel Emma Sullivan, "When Water-Cooler Chats Aren't Enough," *The Wall Street Journal*, May 1, 2013, p. B6; Max Nisen, "Zappos to Build Intentionally Inconvenient Office in Las Vegas, Arch Daily, March 28, 2013; Ben Kesling and James R. Hagerty, "Say Goodbye to the Office Cubicle," *The Wall Street Journal*, April 2, 2013.
7. Joe Light, "Finance and Tech Signal Bold Attitudes on Ethics," *The Wall Street Journal*, March 7, 2011.
8. Lisa Magloff, "Examples of Transformational Change," *Chron*; Nokia, "The Nokia Story".
9. Adam Smith, *Wealth of Nations* (New York: Modern Library, 1937; originally published in 1776).
10. Malcolm Moore, "What Has Triggered the Suicide Cluster at Foxconn?" *The Telegraph*, May 16, 2010.
11. Unilever, "Annual Report and Accounts 2013".
12. PepsiCo Inc., *The New York Times*, March 31, 2014. PepsiCo Inc., "Global Business Units".
13. Diageo, "Regions".
14. Procter & Gamble, "P&G Organizes Global Business Units into Industry-Based Sectors," *P&G Corporate Newsroom*, June 5, 2013.
15. Micah Solomon, "Take These Two Steps to Rival Nordstrom's Customer Service Experience," *Forbes*, March 15, 2014.
16. Kerry Hannon, "The Write Stuff," *Money*, October 2013, pp. 29–30; Nota Bene, "About Us"; "Nota Bene," *Whirl Magazine*, June 9, 2010; "Shopping Guide," *Pittsburgh Magazine*.
17. Julie Jargon, "Burger King Joins Crowd in India," *The Wall Street Journal*, November 19, 2014; Lily Kuo, "Why Burger King Should Sell Pizza at Its New Restaurants in India," *Quartz*, November 21, 2013.
18. "Why Work Here?".
19. PR Newswire, "PepsiCo Unveils New Organizational Structure, Names CEOs of Three Principle Operating Units," November 5, 2007; "The PepsiCo Family," PepsiCo.
20. Jon R. Katzenbach and Douglas K. Smith, "The Discipline of Teams," *Harvard Business Review*, 71 (March–April 1993), p. 19.
21. Ibid.
22. John Baldoni, "The Secret to Team Collaboration: Individuality," *Inc*., January 18, 2012.
23. Gregory Ciotti, "Why Remote Teams Are the Future (and How to Make Them Work)," *Help Scout*, October 23, 2013.
24. Esther Shein, "Making the Virtual Team Real," *The Network*, April 2, 2008.
25. Patrick Kiger, "Task Force Training Develops New Leaders, Solves Real Business Issues and Helps Cut Costs," *Workforce*, September 7, 2011; Duane D. Stanford, "Coca-Cola Woman Board Nominee Bucks Slowing Diversity Trend," *Bloomberg*, February 22, 2013.
26. Jerry Useem, "What's That Spell? TEAMWORK," *Fortune*, June 12, 2006, p. 66.
27. Jia Lynnyang, "The Power of Number 4.6," *Fortune*, June 12, 2006, p. 122.
28. Natasha Singer, "Intel's Sharp-Eyed Social Scientist," *The New York Times*, February 15, 2014.
29. Catherine Dunn, "Brother-and-Sister Brewer," *Fortune*, November 18, 2013; Esha Chhabra, "Fair Trade Crucial Ingredient in Numi Organic Teas," *SF Gate*, December 30, 2011; Certified B Corporation, "Numi Organic Tea"; Kristen, "Numi Organic Tea Brews 'Pure Tea' Precedent with Non-GMO Verification," *The Shelby Report*, August 27, 2012.
30. Richard S. Wellins, William C. Byham, and Jeanne M. Wilson, *Empowered Teams: Creating Self-Directed Work Groups That Improve Quality, Productivity, and Participation* (San Francisco: Jossey-Bass Publishers, 1991), p. 5.
31. Matt Krumrie, "Are Meetings a Waste of Time? Survey Says Yes," *Minneapolis Workplace Examiner*, May 12, 2009.
32. Peter Mell and Timothy Grance, "The NIST Definition of Cloud Computing," National Institute of Standards and Technology, Special Publication 800-145, September 2011.
33. Michael Christian, "Top 10 Ideas: Making the Most of Your Corporate Intranet," April 2, 2009.
34. Kim Komando, "Why You Need a Company Policy on Internet Use".
35. PBSNewsHour, "Apple Supplier Foxconn Pledges Better Working Conditions, but Will It Deliver?" *YouTube*.
36. Michael D. Maginn, *Effective Teamwork*, 1994, p. 10. © 1994 Richard D. Irwin, a Times Mirror Higher Education Group Inc. Company.
37. Tony Hsieh, "Zappos CEO: Training, Mentorship at the Core of Our Employee 'Pipeline Strategy,'" *The Huffington Post*, January 21, 2011; Eleanor Bloxham, "Zappos and the Search for a Better Way to Run a Business," *CNN Money*, January 29, 2014.

Chapter 3

1. Kristie Lu Stout, "How Cirque de Soleil Scouts Clowns, Trapeze Artists and Gymnasts," CNN, September 12, 2012; Mehrdad Baghai and James Quigley, "Cirque de Soleil: A Very

Different Vision of Teamwork," book excerpt from *As One: Individual Action, Collective Power, reprinted* in *Fast Company*, February 4, 2011; Cirque du Soleil Jobs website.

2. "About O*NET," O*NET Resource Center.
3. "P&G Careers".
4. U.S. Department of Health and Human Services, "Results from the 2010 National Survey on Drug Use and Health: Summary of National Findings," September 2011.
5. "Substance Abuse Costs Employers Billions," *The National Registry of Workers' Compensation Specialists*.
6. Manuel Valdes and Shannon McFarland, "Job Seekers' Facebook Password Asked for During U.S. Interviews," *Huffington Post*, March 20, 2012.
7. Jonathan Dame, "Will Employers Still Ask for Facebook Passwords in 2014?" *USA Today*, January 10, 2014.
8. Allison Linn, "Desperate Measures: Why Some People Fake Their Resumes," *CNBC*, February 7, 2014; "Martoma Trial: Ex-SAC Trader Was Expelled by Harvard," *CNBC*, January 10, 2014.
9. Christopher T. Marquet and Lisa J. B. Peterson, "Résumé Fraud: The Top Ten Lies," Marquet International, Ltd..
10. U.S. Equal Employment Opportunity Commission, "Charge Statistics FY 1997 Through FY 2013"; U.S. Equal Employment Opportunity Commission, "Sexual Harassment Charges FY 2010–FY 2013".
11. Bryce Covert, "Only White, Male CEOs Make the Big Bucks," *Think Progress*, October 22, 2013; Alliance for Board Diversity Census, "Missing Pieces: Women and Minorities on Fortune 500 Boards," 2012.
12. "Compulsory Retirement Age at 65 Fully Abolished," *BBC News*, October 1, 2011; "Can You Legally Force Someone to Retire or Is It Age Discrimination?" LawInfo blog.
13. Stephen Bastien, "12 Benefits of Hiring Older Workers," *Entrepreneur.com*, September 20, 2006.
14. Bureau of Labor Statistics, "Usual Weekly Earnings of Wage and Salary Workers First Quarter 2014," April 17, 2014.
15. "Gender and Pay at Work," PayScale.
16. Catherine Rampell, "The Gender Wage Gap, Around the World," March 9, 2010.
17. "Our Curriculum," Hamburger University.
18. "100 Best Companies to Work for 2011," *Fortune*, February 7, 2011.
19. Doug Stewart, "Employee-Appraisal Software," *Inc.*.
20. Maury A. Peiperl, "Getting 360-Degree Feedback Right," *Harvard Business Review*, January 2001, pp. 142–48.
21. Chris Musselwhite, "Self Awareness and the Effective Leader," Inc.com.
22. Rebecca Vesely, "Companies Aim to Improve Wellness of Telecommuting, Traveling Employees, Too," *Workforce*, October 30, 2012.
23. Marcia Zidle, "Employee Turnover: Seven Reasons Why People Quit Their Jobs," Alrakoba.
24. Scott Neuman, "RadioShack to Close 1,000 Stores Nationwide Amid Big Losses," *NPR*, March 4, 2014.
25. Kevin Doyle, "Job Market Sees Growing Demand for Sustainability Managers," *Experience*, 2008; Oliver Balch, "How to Get a Career in Sustainability: Hard Work, Talent, and Perseverance," *The Guardian*, October 9, 2013; Andrew Martin, "In Eco-Friendly Factory, Low-Guilt Potato Chips," *The New York Times*, November 15, 2007.
26. "Wage and Hour Division (WHD)," U.S. Department of Labor.
27. Lauren Fox, "Democrats Push to Pass Minimum Wage Hike Ahead of 2014 Elections," *U.S. News*, April 28, 2014.
28. "Fair Labor Standards Act Advisor," U.S. Department of Labor.
29. City of Santa Fe, "Santa Fe's Living Wage Rises to $10.66 an Hour on March 1, 2014," January 22, 2014; New Mexico Department of Workforce Solutions, "Minimum Wage Information"; Daniel J. Chacón, "Minimum-Wage Workers in City to See Pay Rise to $10.66," *Santa Fe New Mexican*, January 22, 2014.
30. "Kele & Co: First Innovative Jewelry Company in Direct Sales," May 5, 2008; Kele & Co., "About Kele & Co," 2010.
31. Sarah Anderson, "Wall Street's 2013 Bonuses Were More Than All Workers Earned Making the Federal Minimum," *Moyers & Company*, March 12, 2014.
32. The National Center for Employee Ownership, "ESOP (Employee Stock Ownership Plan) Facts," 2014.
33. Bureau of Labor Statistics, "Employer Costs for Employee Compensation," March 12, 2014.
34. Stephan Miller, "Employee Loyalty Hits 7-Year Low; Benefits Promote Retention," *Society for Human Resource Management*, March 22, 2012.
35. "Work/Life," Lowe's.
36. Elaine Pofeldt, "Having Trouble Finding Talent? Look Beyond Resumes," *Inc.*, November 2013; Urban Lending Solutions, "About Us"; Paul J. Gough, "*Inc.* Honors Urban Lending Solutions as Top Job-Creator," *Pittsburg Business Times*, December 6, 2012.
37. Bureau of Labor Statistics, "Union Members Summary," January 24, 2014.
38. Josh Eidelson, "Walmart Fires Eleven Strikers in Alleged Retaliation," *The Nation*, June 22, 2013; Carlyn Kolker, "U.S. Labor Board May Issue Complaint Against Wal-Mart on Strikes," *Reuters*, November 18, 2013; Dave Jamieson, "Feds Charge Walmart with Breaking Labor Law in Black Friday Strikes," *Huffington Post*, January 25, 2014.
39. Steven Greenhouse, "Labor Battle at Kellogg Plant in Memphis Drags On," *The New York Times*, February 10, 2014.
40. Ed Stoddard and Zandi Shabalala, "Producers, Union to Meet Mediator Separately in Platinum Strike," *Reuters*, February 10, 2014.
41. Paul M. Barrett, "Chevron Inches Closer to Legal Victory over Ecuador Pollution," *Bloomberg Businessweek*,

September 19, 2013.

42. Eric Kayne, "Census: White Majority in U.S. Gone by 2043," *NBC News*, June 13, 2013.
43. Press Release, "Kaiser Permanente Named No. 4 on DiversityInc's Top 50 Companies for Diversity List for 2014," Kaiser Permanente, April 24, 2014.
44. Melanie Tervalon, "At a Decade: Centers of Excellence in Culturally Competent Care," *The Permanente Journal*, 13, no. 1 (2009), pp. 87–91.
45. Taylor H. Cox, Jr., "The Multicultural Organization," *Academy of Management Executives* 5 (May 1991), pp. 34–47; Marilyn Loden and Judy B. Rosener, *Workforce America! Managing Employee Diversity as a Vital Resource* (Homewood, IL: Business One Irwin, 1991).
46. Jean Eaglesham and Michael Rothfeld, "Wall Street vs. Its Employees' Privacy," *The Wall Street Journal*, April 22, 2013, p. A1; Jennifer Van Grove, "Securities Regulators Balk at Employee Social Media Privacy," *CNet*, April 22, 2013; Rachel Emma Silverman, "Facebook and Twitter Postings Cost CFO His Job," *The Wall Street Journal*, May 14, 2012.
47. Kathryn Brenzel, "Taco Hell: Lawsuit against Food Truck Claims Employee Was Overworked without Pay," *NJ.com*, December 9, 2013; Dave Jamieson, "More Amazon Warehouse Workers Sue Retailer over Unpaid Security Waits," *The Huffington Post*, September 19, 2013; Dave Jamieson, "Join the Booming Dollar Store Economy! Low Pay, Long Hours, May Work While Injured," *Huffington Post*, August 29, 2013.
48. Paul Davidson, "Overworked and Underpaid?" *USA Today*, April 16, 2012, pp. 1A–2A.
49. Ibid.
50. Melanie Trottman, "For Angry Employees, Legal Cover for Rants," *The Wall Street Journal*, December 2, 2011.
51. Martin Crutsinger, "Hiring Grows as Companies Hit Limits with Workers," *MPR News*, March 7, 2012.
52. Actors Equity Association, "Equity Timeline," Actors Equity, 2006; Writers Guild of America, West, Inc., "History," Writers Guild of America, West, 2012; Jonathon Mandell, "Recalling 1988 Strike," *CBS News*, February 11, 2009; Screen Actors Guild, "History," SAG-AFTRA One Union, 2012; Richard Verrier, "SAG and AFTRA Members Give Thumbs Up to Merger," *Los Angeles Times*, March 30, 2012.

Glossary 术语表

A

accountability the principle that employees who accept an assignment and the authority to carry it out are answerable to a superior for the outcome.

affirmative action programs legally mandated plans that try to increase job opportunities for minority groups by analyzing the current pool of workers, identifying areas where women and minorities are underrepresented, and establishing specific hiring and promotion goals, with target dates, for addressing the discrepancy.

arbitration settlement of a labor/management dispute by a third party whose solution is legally binding and enforceable.

B

behavior modification changing behavior and encouraging appropriate actions by relating the consequences of behavior to the behavior itself.

benefits nonfinancial forms of compensation provided to employees, such as pension plans, health insurance, paid vacation and holidays, and the like.

bonuses monetary rewards offered by companies for exceptional performance as incentives to further increase productivity.

boycott an attempt to keep people from purchasing the products of a company.

C

centralized organization a structure in which authority is concentrated at the top, and very little decision-making authority is delegated to lower levels.

classical theory of motivation theory suggesting that money is the sole motivator for workers.

collective bargaining the negotiation process through which management and unions reach an agreement about compensation, working hours, and working conditions for the bargaining unit.

commission an incentive system that pays a fixed amount or a percentage of the employee's sales.

commitee a permanent, formal group that performs a specific task.

compressed workweek a four-day (or shorter) period during which an employee works 40 hours.

conciliation a method of outside resolution of labor and management differences in which a third party is brought in to keep the two sides talking.

customer departmentalization the arrangement of jobs around the needs of various types of customers.

D

decentralized organization an organization in which decision-making authority is delegated as far down the chain of command as possible.

delegation of authority giving employees not only tasks, but also the power to make commitments, use resources, and take whatever actions are necessary to carry out those tasks.

departmentalization the grouping of jobs into working units usually called departments, units, groups, or divisions.

development training that augments the skills and knowledge of managers and professionals.

diversity the participation of different ages, genders, races, ethnicities, nationalities, and abilities in the workplace.

E

equity theory an assumption that how much people are willing to contribute to an organization depends on their assessment of the fairness, or equity, of the rewards they will receive in exchange.

esteem needs the need for respect—both self-respect and respect from others.

expectancy theory the assumption that motivation depends not only on how much a person wants something but also on how likely he or she is to get it.

extrinsic rewards benefits and/or recognition received from someone else.

F

flextime a program that allows employees to choose their starting and ending times, provided that they are at work during a specified core period.

functional departmentalization the grouping of jobs that perform similar functional activities, such as finance, manufacturing, marketing, and human resources.

G

geographical departmentalization the grouping of jobs according to geographic location, such as state, region, country, or continent.

grapevine an informal channel of communication, separate from management's formal, official communication channels.

group two or more individuals who communicate with one another, share a common identity, and have a common goal.

H

human relations the study of the behavior of individuals and groups in organizational settings.

human resources management (HRM) all the activities involved in determining an organization's human resources needs, as well as acquiring, training, and compensating people to fill those needs.

hygiene factors aspects of Herzberg's theory of motivation that focus on the work setting and not the content of the work; these aspects include adequate wages, comfortable and safe working conditions, fair company policies, and job security.

I

intrinsic rewards the personal satisfaction and enjoyment felt after attaining a goal.

J

job analysis the determination, through observation and study, of pertinent information about a job—including specific tasks and necessary abilities, knowledge, and skills.

job description a formal, written explanation of a specific job, usually including job title, tasks, relationship with other jobs, physical and mental skills required, duties, responsibilities, and working conditions.

job enlargement the addition of more tasks to a job instead of treating each task as separate.

job enrichment the incorporation of motivational factors, such as opportunity for achievement, recognition, responsibility, and advancement, into a job.

job rotation movement of employees from one job to another in an effort to relieve the boredom often associated with job specialization.

job sharing performance of one full-time job by two people on part-time hours.

job specification a description of the qualifications necessary for a specific job, in terms of education, experience, and personal and physical characteristics.

L

labor contract the formal, written document that spells out the relationship between the union and management for a specified period of time—usually two or three years.

labor unions employee organizations formed to deal with employers for achieving better pay, hours, and working conditions.

line–and–staff structure a structure having a traditional line relationship between superiors and subordinates and also specialized managers—called staff managers—who are available to assist line managers.

line structure the simplest organizational structure, in which direct lines of authority extend from the top manager to the lowest level of the organization.

lockout management's version of a strike, wherein a work site is closed so that employees cannot go to work.

M

marketing strategy a plan of action for developing, pricing, distributing, and promoting products that meet the needs of specific customers.

maslow´s hierarchy a theory that arranges the five basic needs of people—physiological, security, social, esteem, and self-actualization—into the order in which people strive to satisfy them.

matrix structure a structure that sets up teams from different departments, thereby creating two or more intersecting lines of authority; also called a projectmanagement structure.

mediation a method of outside resolution of labor and management differences in which the third party's role is to suggest or propose a solution to the problem.

morale an employee's attitude toward his or her job, employer, and colleagues.

motivation an inner drive that directs a person's behavior toward goals.

motivational factors aspects of Herzberg's theory of motivation that focus on the content of the work itself; these aspects include achievement, recognition, involvement, responsibility, and advancement.

multidivisional structure a structure that organizes departments into larger groups called divisions.

O

organizational chart a visual display of the organizational structure, lines of authority (chain of command), staff relationships, permanent committee arrangements, and lines of communication.

organizational culture a firm's shared values, beliefs, traditions, philosophies, rules, and role models for behavior.

organizational layers the levels of management in an organization.

orientation familiarizing newly hired employees with fellow workers, company procedures, and the physical properties of the company.

P

physiological needs the most basic human needs to be satisfied—water, food, shelter, and clothing.

picketing a public protest against management practices that involves union members marching and carrying antimanagement signs at the employer's plant.

product departmentalization the organization of jobs in relation to the products of the firm.

product-development teams a specific type of project team formed to devise, design, and implement a new product.

profit sharing a form of compensation whereby a percentage of company profits is distributed to the employees whose work helped to generate them.

project teams groups similar to task forces that normally run their operation and have total control of a specific work project.

promotion an advancement to a higher-level job with increased authority, responsibility, and pay.

Q

quality-assurance teams (or quality circles) small groups of workers brought together from throughout the organization to solve specific quality, productivity, or service problems.

R

recruiting forming a pool of qualified applicants from which management can select employees.

responsibility the obligation, placed on employees through delegation, to perform assigned tasks satisfactorily and be held accountable for the proper execution of work.

S

salary a financial reward calculated on a weekly, monthly, or annual basis.

security needs the need to protect oneself from physical and economic harm.

selection the process of collecting information about applicants and using that information to make hiring decisions.

self-actualization needs the need to be the best one can be; at the top of Maslow's hierarchy.

self-directed work team (SDWT) a group of employees responsible for an entire work process or segment that delivers a product to an internal or external customer.

separations employment changes involving resignation, retirement, termination, or layoff.

social needs the need for love, companionship, and friendship—the desire for acceptance by others.

span of management the number of subordinates who report to a particular manager.

specialization the division of labor into small, specific tasks and the assignment of employees to do a single task.

strikebreakers people hired by management to replace striking employees; called "scabs" by striking union members.

strikes employee walkouts; one of the most effective weapons labor has.

structure the arrangement or relationship of positions within an organization.

T

task force a temporary group of employees responsible for bringing about a particular change.

team a small group whose members have complementary skills; have a common purpose, goals, and approach; and hold themselves mutually accountable.

Theory X McGregor's traditional view of management whereby it is assumed that workers generally dislike work and must be forced to do their jobs.

Theory Y McGregor's humanistic view of management whereby it is assumed that workers like to work and that under proper conditions employees will seek out responsibility in an attempt to satisfy their social, esteem, and self-actualization needs.

Theory Z a management philosophy that stresses employee participation in all aspects of company decision making.

Title VII of the Civil Rights Act prohibits discrimination in employment and created the Equal Employment Opportunity Commission.

training teaching employees to do specific job tasks through either classroom development or on-the-job experience.

transfer a move to another job within the company at essentially the same level and wage.

turnover occurs when employees quit or are fired and must be replaced by new employees.

W

wage/salary survey a study that tells a company how much compensation comparable firms are paying for specific jobs that the firms have in common.

wages financial rewards based on the number of hours the employee works or the level of output achieved.

Photo Credits 图片版权

Chapter 1 Opener: © Charles Eshelman/Getty Images; p. 4: © BananaStock/PunchStock; p. 5: © jas0420/iStock; p. 8: © Image Source/Getty Images; p. 15: © nyul/iStock; p. 18: © Jetta Productions/Getty Images; p. 20: © ColorBlind Images/Getty Images.

Chapter 2 Opener: © Zuma Press/Newscom; p. 29: © Michael Orrell/The El Dorado News-Times/AP Images; p. 32: © Ulrich Baumgarten/Getty Images; p. 44: © Stuart Isett/Polaris/Newscom; p. 46: © NetPhotos/Alamy. Teijeiro/Getty Images.

Chapter 3 Opener: © Kris Connor/Getty Images; p. 56: © Digital Vision/Getty Images; p. 58: © Onsite/Alamy; p. 61: © Kirby Hamilton/iStock; p. 65: © Tannen Maury/Bloomberg via Getty Images; p. 66: © Eric Audras/Getty Images; p. 67: © JGI/Jamie Grill/Getty Images; p.71: © Mark Bowden/iStock; p. 78: © Beathan/Corbis.